# JEWISH STUDIES

**Key Words in Jewish Studies**

*Series Editors*
Deborah Dash Moore, University of Michigan
Macdonald Moore, University of Michigan
Andrew Bush, Vassar College

1. Andrew Bush, *Jewish Studies*

# JEWISH STUDIES

*A Theoretical Introduction*

ANDREW BUSH

RUTGERS UNIVERSITY PRESS

*New Brunswick, New Jersey, and London*

Library of Congress Cataloging-in-Publication Data

Bush, Andrew, 1954 Apr. 19–

Jewish studies : a theoretical introduction / Andrew Bush.

    p. cm.—(Key words in Jewish studies ; v. 1)

  Includes bibliographical references and index.

  ISBN 978–0-8135–4954–5 (hardcover : alk. paper)

  1. Judaism—Study and teaching (Higher) 2. Jews—Study and teaching (Higher)
I. Title.

  BM71.B88  2011

  296.071—dc22

2010021013

A British Cataloging-in-Publication record for this book is available from the British Library.

Visit our Web site: http://rutgerspress.rutgers.edu

Manufactured in the United States of America

*To, for, and with Olga*

# Contents

# Foreword

The Rutgers University Press series Key Words in Jewish Studies seeks to introduce students and scholars alike to vigorous developments in the field by exploring its terms. These words and phrases reference important concepts, issues, practices, events, and circumstances. But terms also refer to standards, even to preconditions; they patrol the boundaries of the field of Jewish Studies. This series aims to transform outsiders into insiders and let insiders gain new perspectives on usages, some of which shift even as we apply them.

Key words mutate through repetition, suppression, amplification, and competitive sharing. Jewish Studies finds itself attending to such processes in the context of an academic milieu where terms are frequently repurposed. Diaspora offers an example of an ancient word, one with a specific Jewish resonance, which has traveled into new regions and usage. Such terms migrate from the religious milieu of Jewish learning to the secular environment of universities, from Jewish community discussion to arenas of academic discourse, from political debates to intellectual arguments and back again. As these key words travel, they acquire additional meanings even as they occasionally shed long-established connotations. On occasion, key words can become so politicized that they serve as accusations. The sociopolitical concept of assimilation, for example, when turned into a term—assimilationist—describing an advocate of the process among Jews, became an epithet hurled by political opponents struggling for the mantle of authority in Jewish communities.

When approached dispassionately, key words provide analytical leverage to expand debate in Jewish Studies. Some key words will be familiar from long use, and yet they may have gained new valences, attracting or repelling other terms in contemporary discussion. But there are prominent terms in Jewish culture whose key lies in a particular understanding of prior usage. Terms of the past may bolster claims to continuity in the present while newly minted language sometimes disguises deep connections reaching back into history. Attention must be paid as well to the transmigration of key words among Jewish languages—especially Hebrew, Yiddish, and Ladino—and among languages used by Jews, knitting connections even while highlighting distinctions.

An exploration of the current state of Jewish Studies through its key words highlights some interconnections often only glimpsed and holds out the prospect of a reorganization of Jewish knowledge. Key words act as magnets and attract a nexus of ideas and arguments as well as related terms into their orbits. This series plunges into several of these intersecting constellations, providing a path from past to present.

The volumes in the series share a common organization. They open with a first section, Terms of Debate, which defines the key word as it developed over the course of Jewish history. Allied concepts and traditional terms appear here as well. The second section, State of the Question, analyzes contemporary debates in scholarship and popular venues, especially for those key words that have crossed over into popular culture. The final section, In a New Key, explicitly addresses contemporary culture and future possibilities for understanding the key word.

To decipher key words is to learn the varied languages of Jewish Studies at points of intersection between academic disciplines and wider spheres of culture. The series, then, does not seek to consolidate and narrow a particular critical lexicon. Its purpose is to question, not to canonize, and to invite readers to sample the debate and ferment of an exciting field of study.

Andrew Bush
Deborah Dash Moore
MacDonald Moore
Series Editors

# Acknowledgments

Julie and Gus opened their doors and set a table by the window for break-fast and conversation. At first, Deborah Dash Moore and I would meet there to prepare the seminars that we were teaching together in Jewish Studies, and soon MacDonald Moore joined us. Those conversations formed part of a larger effort by dedicated colleagues and students to create a full Jewish Studies program at Vassar College, finally founded in 2000, and eventually led to the formulation of this book series, Key Words in Jewish Studies, which this volume introduces. All the thinking and many of the analytical and theoretical discussions presented here were first articulated in my undergraduate Jewish Studies classes at Vassar, and my gratitude to my students for engaging in this work with me is beyond measure.

When Deborah and Mac moved on to the Frankel Center for Jewish Studies at the University of Michigan, the generous support of the Padnos family made it possible for me to spend a semester there as the Padnos Scholar in Residence, and so to renew our discussions and produce a preliminary draft of this text in the company of the dear friends who helped to initiate the project and who remain a constant inspiration. Conversation on comparative religion with Peter Leonard, philosopher and Vassar's director of field work (an unusual combination), at the deli just a few doors up from Julie's was another essential support as I moved beyond my home department of Hispanic Studies and various other com-mitments in Vassar's lively array of multidisciplinary programs to my consistent professional involvement in Jewish Studies. Just down the block, conversations with Himadeep Muppidi and Andrew Davison, pro-fessors of political science, at Ken's Crafted Kup and John Henry Davis over at Walter's Three Arts bookstore were especially helpful in thinking through the political dimensions of scholarship. The places in town and in the text where I have met with Anne Gordan and Mihai Grünfeld are many. A particular discussion with Andy when I was at a very low ebb in the work proved absolutely decisive in enabling me to continue. It takes a village to write a book, and a bookstore to make a village, and the center of my village is Julie's.

My growth in the field of Jewish Studies and indeed the growth of the Jewish Studies Program at Vassar are also greatly indebted to the generosity of alumna Suzanne Fishman and her husband, Dr. Lawrence Fishman, who have made it possible to organize the annual Fishman Faculty Development Seminar. Many of our seminar leaders are noted in these pages; all have been important to my exploration of the field; and among them, Riv-Ellen Prell and Jonathan Boyarin have also been generous in their responses to this book project. I have also been fortunate to receive financial support from the Littauer Fund of Vassar's Jewish Studies Program to meet some of the expenses of publication.

The book has been fashioned in a series of related but fairly independent drafts, each composed quickly, followed by substantial periods of reflection that were motivated by the judicious responses of a small group of readers. Mac and Deborah read most of those drafts in full; Andy read one and Jonathan another. But above all, before and beyond the village, I have written this book in the midst of a family of readers. My father had read very nearly every word that I have written since my report on Robert Frost in sixth grade, if not earlier. Responding to the manuscript of my first book, he discovered in its hundreds of pages the three lines that meant most to me and encouraged me to rethink my project from that place, which I did. When I sent him the first draft of this new manuscript, he read and commented, as always, but also insisted that the time had come to pass the editorial baton. Conversation with my son Sasha was crucial in finding that same place in this work, enabling me to move from what Bernard Malamud has called the stage of improving the prose to that of saying what must still be said. My brothers Harley and Michael read and commented on one draft, and my son Daniel worked through several line by line. Their contributions, and the support of the rest of the family—first and foremost my mother, and Iosif, Alec and Rita, Vicki and Anthony, Nedra, Alyssa, Matt, Brett and Shira—have made this effort by a relative newcomer to the field of Jewish Studies into, quite literally, a labor, and a history, of love.

I reserve a note apart for Olga Bush, to whom this book is dedicated, for whom I wrote it, and with whom I have weighed every page, looking for the cadence, the balance, the missing word, the key. Together, for thirty years of marriage, building a Jewish life.

# JEWISH STUDIES

# Introduction

## To What May This Be Likened?

### Studying Jews

When German Jewish philosopher Franz Rosenzweig inaugurated an experimental program in Jewish adult education in Frankfurt in 1920, he framed the project as a question of *learning*. He qualified his key word: "Learning," he wrote, "there are by now, I should say, very few among you unable to catch the curious note the word sounds, even today, when it is used in a Jewish context."[1] He expected that his audience could hear the word "learning" twice—more precisely, most of his audience, since he did not impose his hearing test as a criterion for admission to the new institute. First, in plain German, his audience, schooled in the principles of modern education, would understand learning as a freely chosen process of obtaining knowledge primarily for the purposes of self-betterment. But he expected that most would also overhear the term "learning" to designate "the old form of maintaining the relationship between life and the Book."[2] It is in this older, Jewish sense that, more than a century later, contemporary scholar of classical Judaism Jacob Neusner still uses the term "learning Jews" to characterize the early rabbis.[3]

In contrast to learning Jews, *studying Jews* represents what anthropologist Talal Asad calls "a change in the grammar of a concept."[4] Learning Jews are the subjects of a practice; they are Jews who learn. More particularly, they are Jews for whom the practice of learning is the fulfillment of a covenantal obligation. For it is the curious note of learning in a Jewish context—curious from the point of view of the modern university—that one is commanded to learn; and that one learns not to know, but to do; and to do what God commands. Studying Jews, on the contrary, has meant taking Jews and what they do as an object of study, for the purpose of producing, testing, and disseminating knowledge about Jews, regardless of who happens to be doing the studying. The fundamental question for studying Jews is not how to maintain a relationship to the Jewish God, to the Jewish Book, or to the Jewish people, but what kind of object does one study when studying Jews? A religious group? A nation? A race? A personal or collective identity? A paradigmatic or historical Other?

The nomenclature for *Jewish* Studies varies according to local institutional histories—sometimes Judaic Studies, Near Eastern Studies, and other possibilities—but it is rather the change from Jewish *Learning* to Jewish *Studies* that constitutes a new view of the relationship between Jewish lives and certain books, life practices, and material culture. Inasmuch as those who happen to be studying Jews have often been Jews themselves, that new relationship and its attendant practices have become an important element of some Jewish lives. Thus, Jewish Studies is itself one of the phenomena that the field has been constituted to investigate. Hence, this book, whose key word is "Jewish Studies."

And yet the new does not supersede the old, but transforms it. Sociologist of religion Danièle Hervieu-Léger theorizes that transformative process under the heading of *metaphorization*, as an explicit alternative to the concept of *secularization*. "Far from being an indication of the disintegration of religion in societies where politics, science, art, sexuality, and culture have gradually broken free from the control of traditional religions," she writes, "metaphorization testifies to the fact that their new autonomy has made them available for a new kind of religious function; and it needs be asked how this function compares with that performed by traditional religions in premodern society."[5] It is in much the same way, and informed, in part, by the same social science tradition, that philosopher of Judaism Rabbi Mordecai Kaplan characterized the transformation of *mitzvoth*, commandments, in modern Jewish life a generation earlier: "Even though some of us no longer regard the traditional practices as commanded by God, we may still refer to them as [mitzvoth], provided we avowedly use that term in a metaphorical sense."[6] Kaplan refers most immediately to the evocation of a "religious mood," a much contested concept; but more broadly, the metaphorical extension that he both explicates and promotes is a displacement. As opposed to an evacuation of the sacred—a "disenchantment" of life in Weberian terms—such as one would expect under the heading of secularization, Kaplan shifts the focus. Jewish tradition had always recognized the sacred in holy God, holy Book, and holy people. Living and writing in the United States in the 1930s, Kaplan came to emphasize the last of those three pillars, centering Jewish religious experience in Jewish peoplehood, such that Jewish "folkways" (his period language), inasmuch as they promoted solidarity within Jewish communities and between the present and the past, took on religious force. The folkways were, metaphorically, commandments authored and authorized by the people.

Needless to say, Kaplan's self-conscious program of reconstruction did not meet with universal acceptance as a mode of religious devotion among Jews in the United States or anywhere else. Yet the broader cultural processes combining displacement and retention of the sacred in the life practices and self-expression of Jews have been widespread. Thus, literary critic Dan Miron writes of "the metaphorization of the literary image of the shtetl," that is, the townlets that were Jewish population centers in Eastern Europe, in classical fictional narratives in Hebrew and in Yiddish in the late nineteenth and early twentieth century.[7] The imagination of the shtetl, Miron explains, is "structured around a metaphorical-conceptual core. . . . The shtetl was Jerusalem in her fallen state, and yet it was still Jerusalem—the Jewish polity par excellence."[8] The shtetl, in its literary depiction, is like and is not Jerusalem, to recall the elucidation of the work of metaphor by philosopher Paul Ricoeur.[9] Is not: the shtetl was not the Chosen Place, site of the Holy of Holies in the Temple; and despite the fact that the fictional shtetl, contrary to its historical counterpart, was made over into an all but entirely Jewish space, it was not an area of Jewish political autonomy, as the ancient kingdom had been. Is like: the Judaized shtetl of fiction (its non-Jewish population and attendant institutions largely hidden from view) represented a cohesive and distinct Jewish domain, and with it an image of Jews as a people apart—which is to say, metaphorically, a holy people.

This process of metaphorization in Jewish culture is evident in Jewish Studies as well. To remain for the moment in the same milieu, one may turn to the great pioneering figure of modern Jewish ethnography, S. Ansky (Shloyme-Zanvl Rappoport). Literary critic David G. Roskies declares that Ansky "identified Jewish folklore with the Oral Torah itself," which is to say with the parallel revelation to Moses at Sinai transmitted orally and ultimately compiled in the canonical texts of rabbinic Judaism.[10] Folklore is clearly Oral Torah only metaphorically, for neither Ansky nor Roskies claims that along with mishnaic dicta, grandma's tales and recipes were handed down to and through Moses. But the force of the metaphor likening the stories, music, and artifacts collected by Ansky to holy law, much as the narratives of S. Y. Abramovitsh and Sholem Rabinovitsh (popularly known as Mendele Moykher Sforim and Sholem Aleichem, respectively) likened the shtetl to holy land, serves to displace the salient elements of Jewish distinctiveness from divine commandments articulated in the Written and Oral Torah to the lived experience of Jewish people. The intellectual move is typical of the field. For nearly two centuries, Jewish Studies has meant, above all, studying Jews.

Roskies maps Ansky's particular case onto a more general "paradigm of return" in modern Jewish culture, whereby Jews estranged from Jewish learning and its cultural milieu make deliberate efforts to rediscover, reinforce, and reassert their links to the Jewish people. Ansky not only sought to accomplish such a return for himself when he determined to bring his

training in other disciplines to bear upon the study of Jews, but also saw
the work of Jewish Studies as a crucial, even a necessary element in promoting the same path for others: "[He] did not intend for 'assimilated'
Jews to return to 'traditional' ways of life, but rather to create knowledge
that would make possible new forms of Jewish identity, which would
regenerate the Jews as a people."[11] Sectarian Jewish institutions, such as
synagogues and Jewish community centers, continue to embrace Jewish
Studies—in the form of adult education courses, for instance, including
those of Rosenzweig's institute in Frankfurt—precisely for the purpose of
enhancing a sense of belonging.

It is almost needless to say that in nonsectarian universities the field of
Jewish Studies does not espouse that goal, especially since, more like the
historical shtetl than its fictional image, Jewish Studies programs have
mixed populations of Jews and non-Jews. It is not the purpose of Jewish
Studies in the nonsectarian university to make students Jewish or more
Jewish, whatever those expressions might mean. Nevertheless, as Ansky
anticipated and exemplified, for some students the field of Jewish Studies
is itself a path of return without any prerequisite of shared faith or
religious practice. Like the education of the American student majoring
in American literature, or the same student electing a course in Hispanic
Studies and leaving the classroom with greater sensitivity to and respect
for the peoples of Spanish-speaking lands, the strengthening of solidarities
through Jewish Studies between those studying Jews, whoever they are,
and the Jews whom they study contributes to the more general humanistic enterprise of the university.

As an academic field, Jewish Studies has reenacted the intellectual
history of the Western universities where it has come to find a home.
The university undertook to remove intellectual life from the authority of
the Church; Jewish Studies has also separated the study of Jews from the
religious authority governing Jewish learning. It is a concomitant of this
conception of Jewish Studies as an academic pursuit that work in the field
is generally conducted through the methodologies of disciplines found
elsewhere in the university (e.g., philosophy, sociology, literary criticism,
and ethnography, to enumerate the disciplines that have already been
mentioned briefly and to which, along with history and others, discussion
will return in the chapters to follow).

Yet the reference to Oral Torah as a metaphor for Jewish folkways as
reconstructed through Ansky's research points to self-conscious efforts to
liken Jewish Studies nonetheless to Jewish learning. It is a less consistent
practice, but Jewish Studies also attempts, at times, to contribute to the
university at large not only by selecting an additional object—Jews—for
study from the perspective of other academic disciplines, marked as they

inevitably are by their cultural and institutional histories, but also by drawing upon the resources of Jewish learning for conceptual tools, analytic methods, and pedagogic metaphors that might articulate an indigenous point of view. In short, Jewish Studies can also serve to reverse the "change in grammar," recognizing the object of study as a subject in its own right, giving voice to Jews in the understanding and articulation of their own historical experience.

## Terms of Debate and State of the Question

The books in the Key Words series, beginning here, are organized in three sections: "Terms of Debate," "State of the Question," and "In a New Key." It is possible to read these headings as an elaboration of the historical divisions of past-present-future. No doubt some of the authors in the series will do so—there is every reason to hope that the continuity of format will throw into relief a diversity of approach. In any case, the present volume is attentive to but not constrained by historical models and methods, and it does not follow an unbroken timeline. So, for instance, the third section of the first chapter, "Terms of Debate," does not extend the chronology reaching roughly from the late eighteenth century to the Second World War, examined in the previous two sections, but rather covers at least part of the same historical period again— re-covers it—from a different point of departure and a different critical angle. The same is true about the relationship between chapter 3 and the first two chapters. The structure of chapter 1, then, anticipates, or encapsulates, the structure of the book as a whole.

"Terms of Debate" begins in Berlin and proceeds to the discussion of such key words as *science, history, nation, race*, and *religion* that orient the predominant formation of Jewish Studies amongst German Jewish scholars and their heirs over the course of the nineteenth century and on to the beginning of the Second World War. Yet standing beyond that vigorous debate, one notes the discrepancy between the universalizing tendency of those key words, in theory, and the Ashkenazi-centric account of the history of Jewish Studies, in practice. It is in that sense that the final section of the chapter steps beyond the well-traveled path of sections one and two, returning to the nineteenth century, questioning Ashkenazi-centrism, and attempting to recover *alterity* in the early history of Jewish Studies.

This move beyond Ashkenaz, too, is a politics in that the theorizing of "other differences" is treated as a call to action. In the following two chapters the effort is made to represent a more balanced geography of Jewish Studies, both with respect to those doing the studying and to the Jews who are studied. Since the same call to action in relation to gender balance guides the discussion from the very first page, this is the place to elucidate its theoretical foundations. A generation of feminist scholarship both within and without Jewish Studies makes it possible to limit explication here to a comment on a parallel case.

In a book that is otherwise an insightful account of the history of modern French historiography, Peter Burke finds no female scholars to discuss among the founders of the *Annales* School in the early twentieth century, his point of departure, or their immediate successors. When he arrives at the third generation, he reports that the legacy has been distributed over a wide array of subfields and methodologies; practical considerations oblige him to choose among them. "The price of this decision," Burke says, "is unfortunately to exclude a good deal of interesting work, notably the contribution to women's history. . . . However, concentration is the only way to prevent this chapter becoming as fragmented as the *Annales* schools is said to be."[12] To choose "concentration" over fragmentation is to promote a theoretical position in the name of an expository strategy. If the reality is fragmented, concentration is tendentious. In practice, Burke's example suggests that if you wait sixty pages to notice Women's Studies, as the history of Jewish Studies is also sometimes told, it might just seem reasonable to continue to leave it out of account from that point forward as well. There is always an alternative expository strategy.

The selection of examples and references becomes part of that strategy here. Needless to say, in a short book it is not possible to mention all the scholarship in a field that takes several millennia as its time span and nearly the whole earth as its geographical domain. The limited choices reflected here do not correspond to an intention to establish an implicit canon of elite quality; they could easily be multiplied many times over and still leave out countless valuable and invaluable topics and contributions. The selection of key words—this too could be extended—guides the selection of topics, and, within those topics, the selection of examples and references seeks to keep the tent pegs stretched as wide as my limited judgment and erudition will allow.[13]

The second chapter takes the Shoah as the point of rupture between the inaugural period of Jewish Studies and the current state of the field, up to and including today. The division serves heuristic purposes, but it is certainly not absolute. Some areas of research offer a straightforward continuation of Jewish Studies as it was practiced in the inaugural period. After all, many of the leading figures in the field in the later twentieth century had begun their own research well before the Second World War. Moreover, as chapter 1 shows, the first hundred years of research in Jewish Studies were not simply homogenous; and the first decades of the twentieth century mark particularly important intellectual changes in the conception and conduct of the field. Nevertheless, like all other aspects of Jewish culture from which the field grows, Jewish Studies is haunted by the near destruction of European Jewry. Most concretely, accomplished and potential scholars in the field were killed, archives and artifacts lost, and whole communities of Jews to be studied were annihilated.

The destruction, and the felt urgency of commitment to the dead, also fomented changes in intellectual orientation that are prevalent up until today. It is the purpose of chapter 2 to highlight those new conceptions by reference to the terms that organize debate in Jewish Studies anew "after Auschwitz"—the expression itself a key word in and for our times. To cite an all but self-evident case, the role of the pseudo-science of "race" in the formation of Nazi ideology and its execution has thoroughly devalued the term in the field of Jewish Studies; *ethnicity* arose in its place. More subtle, and more transformative, the chapter focuses on articulations of *identity* and *memory* in the current state of the question, which contest the hegemony of history in the field in its formative period and mark the growing contributions of psychology and anthropology. Still more recently, formulations of *the Other* contest, in turn, the philosophical and political premises of conceptions of identity.

## In a New Key

"Time forks perpetually toward innumerable futures," writes Argentine storyteller Jorge Luis Borges in "The Garden of Forking Paths."[14] In one of the futures, not in all, there is a sudden burgeoning of Jewish Studies in Buenos Aires and throughout South America, as students of Liberation Theology look more closely into the Jewish sources of Argentine philosopher Enrique Dussel in the writings of Franz Rosenzweig and Emmanuel Lévinas.[15] In another, students of South Asian Subaltern Studies, following the lead of Paul Gilroy's work on the Black Atlantic and the recent arguments of Sander L. Gilman concerning multiculturalism, turn to Jewish Studies for historical precedents and theoretical paradigms pertinent to their analysis of the increasingly diasporic labor force in the world economy.[16] In yet another, Israeli students are welcomed at universities in Syria and Iraq, where they polish their Arabic, leading to a new flourishing in the interpretation of Maimonides. And in a darker future, none of this will matter as the Venetian Ghetto and Manhattan's Lower East Side sink beneath the high tide of global warming, and we are all desperately in search of the world's last glass of drinking water. In sum, the Jewish Studies to come will depend on political developments and material conditions as yet unrealized and so radically unpredictable: "a future that is, at best, inscrutable and, at worst, terminal," in the words of poet and literary critic Charles Bernstein.[17]

And yet I feel that I have a glimpse of the future in the faces of my students, and so in chapter 3 I return to the classroom to outline a new key in Jewish Studies—one of the innumerable possibilities. There are as many pedagogies as there are futures. In one, for which Lévinas's talmudic lessons may serve as an exemplary case, the classroom has many entrances, many beginnings, but no end in sight: teaching and learning "perpetually" or "continually."[18] In my practice—and chapter 3 is an attempt to practice, rather than to describe, a new key in Jewish Studies—this means to place before my students a number of fragments of diverse provenance (disciplinary, historical, geographical, gendered diversity) and to allow the pathways between them to come to light and multiply, to intersect and to change direction, through a process of rereading, which, ideally, keeps all texts virtually open to the readers and to each other. Walter Benjamin— philosopher and literary critic, a theorist for urban studies, film studies, and a host of other multidisciplinary areas, and the principal influence on my own teaching in Jewish Studies—speaks of "the strangest corridors" unexpectedly connecting word and word.[19] I prefer to speak, metaphorically, of a correspondence course, as though all who are studying Jews were writing letters to one another, as though all the texts in Jewish Studies were linked.

As concerns the writing of the third chapter, this means, most literally, that an essay by Rosenzweig in the form of a letter to the philosopher Martin Buber is one of my starting points, and an epistolary exchange between Benjamin and Gershom Scholem, the scholar of Jewish mysticism who was perhaps the most highly esteemed figure in Jewish Studies in the later twentieth century, is another. Rosenzweig takes up pedagogy explicitly. He argues that Buber's openness to transformative practices with respect to Jewish law (that is, metaphorization) needs to be extended to the question of teaching. I have tried to meet that challenge; the key, for me, may be found in Benjamin's pointed exchange with Scholem.

Scholem's long career stretches out considerably on both sides of the historical boundary that I have marked as the dividing point between the first two chapters, namely the Shoah. A direct heir of the first formative century of Jewish Studies, he is also the exemplary figure for the current state of the field in several respects. The originality of his research and the depth of his erudition, the force and reach of his influence, are all unquestionable. But I refer now more particularly to the theoretical position by which he effectively defines (etymologically, sets boundaries to) the field, and thereby also determines research agenda and methods, and even expository strategies. In his correspondence with Benjamin he states his case plainly as a matter of delimiting Jewish Studies by reference to what he calls "Jewish contents."

Scholem's argument for Jewish contents, I note, presupposes that the shape of the container is known in advance. And indeed, a predetermination of the container, frequently expressed as a question of identity in recent years, is most often the starting point, explicit or implicit, of work in Jewish Studies. Some prior understanding of "Jewishness" underwrites a decision about what might pass muster as Jewish contents and so might serve as a pertinent object of study. More vulgarly, the question is posed as "who's a Jew?"—the precise opposite to Rosenzweig's argument for openness, transformation, and the potential for return.

The reader may well feel that I have been begging that question from the outset, when I myself offered my initial gloss on "Jewish Studies" as a key word by suggesting that it is the modern academic discipline of studying Jews. I would counter that this is the question that I am begging not to pose. I learn from Rosenzweig and Lévinas to hold that question perpetually in abeyance. Or to put the matter in the kabbalistic terms that I first learned from Scholem, in this world, the container is broken, the contents, call them sparks of Jewishness, are scattered. It may always have been so. But thinking through the project of Jewish Studies from that perspective may be new.

Benjamin proceeds otherwise than by identifying Jews. He allows for overlapping but non-coincident elements in which some points of intersection (of common experience) are much frequented and others less so, but no particular configuration is to be separated out as authentic, no boundaries define a totality. In the correspondence, Benjamin had argued for that alternative perspective as the elucidation of "Jewish aspects." The term broached in this private conversation never did become a key word in Jewish Studies.

The relation of contents to aspect might be likened to a fuller articulation wherein Benjamin distinguishes, rather, between these and these, this content and that content, specifically, between "material content" and "truth content." He names the researcher into the material content as the commentator and the investigator of truth content as the critic, and explicates their relationship through the simile of a funeral pyre: "the commentator stands before it like a chemist, the critic like an alchemist. Whereas, for the former, wood and ash remain the sole objects of his analysis, for the latter only the flame itself preserves an enigma: that of what is alive."[20] It needs be recognized that the work of the commentator is necessary, particularly in relation to times and places where the funeral pyre has long been extinguished. Indeed, much of Benjamin's own research (most often on contents that no one, himself included, would identify as Jewish) is of this kind: a patient effort to collect the scattered shards of material and textual culture. But it is equally to be recognized that the enigma of the flame, the enigma of living, does not have a prede-termined shape. It is not a contents; it is uncontained. In chapter 3, I have attempted to be both commentator and critic, gathering some few sticks of wood (the forest is endless) and some of the ash, but also trying to glimpse their enigma in the multiple and open interstices between the fragments of material and textual culture.

I would offer another metaphor for this attempt to practice Jewish Studies in a new key, Jewish Studies for which Jewishness is not a prede-termined container, but a question that we are learning to pose. To what may this be likened? To environmental studies, perhaps.

I recall that in its formative period, Jewish Studies developed by artic-ulating a project in relation to the science of the day, much devoted to the isolation of pure strains and the ruling out of extraneous factors. So, too, Jewish Studies in a new key may be related to environmentalism, both a political and a scientific movement that envisions and supports the bal-anced interaction of mixed elements in a complex system whose bound-aries, in principle, may be indefinitely expanded. In chapter 3 I undertake to explore the environment of Jewish modernity.

In practice, I present a set of brief discussions of disparate texts whose most local concerns include such questions as how to approach the future, what is the work of a key, how to appreciate difficulty, what are the alternatives to violence, among other matters pertinent to under-standing what a new key in Jewish Studies might mean. More generally, the fragments consider various modes of human relationship (reader and author, student and teacher, friendship, brotherhood, parents and chil-dren, marriage) as models or metaphors for the correspondence between texts in the complex environment of Jewish culture. Studying Jews means studying such living relationships in perpetual pursuit of their enigma.

To bring the fragments together in a continuous prose exposition would be to presuppose a certain relationship (historical explanation, for instance) and to privilege a certain conclusion. I have preferred a more open form. The points of contact between the fragments vary: sometimes explicit allusion, sometimes common theoretical considerations, some-times shared images or key words. The order of the fragments, if not arbitrary, is not definitive. The pathways between them continue to fork.

I explore a very limited environment in chapter 3. I have selected primarily from among the texts that I have brought with me to under-graduate classes in Jewish Studies. The selections could well be multiplied by as many texts as the reader brings to the conversation. The same must be said of this book as a whole.

# 1 Terms of Debate

## Opening Moves

Two women of the German Jewish middle class meet after a separation of a hundred years in the pages of a book. They offer an opening frame for the period in which the terms of debate in Jewish Studies were forged. One of these women was Hannah Arendt, who would come to be a leading figure in twentieth-century political thought. But in 1929 she had just finished a doctoral dissertation under the direction of one German philosopher and a clandestine love affair with another. The lover, Martin Heidegger, would ride the rising Nazi tide to the rectorship of a German university. His career move serves to highlight, by contrast, Arendt's decision to set aside her dissertation on Saint Augustine and to take up studying Jews. Finished but for the two final chapters when Arendt went into exile from Nazi Germany, the manuscript at last became a book in the United States, in English, in 1958: *Rahel Varnhagen: The Life of a Jewess*.[1]

Arendt would have learned from the model of Saint Augustine that it was possible to conceive of a life allegorically, that is, as two stories at once. For Augustine this meant that the education of the individuated self could represent the unfolding of God's grace. For Arendt, never much interested in the divine, the education of Rahel—as she was known in her lifetime and since, in modern scholarship—could be the vehicle for the examination of Jewish *fate* (the word is Arendt's). "It may well be difficult for us to understand our own history when we are born in 1771 in Berlin and that history has already begun seventeen hundred years earlier in Jerusalem," writes Arendt at the outset of the biography.[2] That dating, which excludes the patriarchal period, as well as the First and Second Temples, makes Jewish history an adjunct of the Christian era. Such a view may well not be difficult at all to understand if you are Rahel, born Levin, but ending your days as Fredericke Varnhagen von Ense—though few students of Jewish Studies would agree. More significant, then, is a different historical continuity that makes it possible for Arendt to discern the beginnings of her own history as a modern Jewish fate dating to the era of Rahel, spanning the late eighteenth and early nineteenth centuries. Arendt's book is allegorical in a second sense, therefore. In telling Rahel's story, she is also telling her own. *Rahel Varnhagen* is Arendt's *Confessions*.

Some scholars, mostly women, have followed Arendt's lead in studying the cultural practice usually referred to as the Berlin Salons, predominantly associated with Jewish women, and with Rahel herself at the
center. The connections with the formation of Jewish Studies, usually
situated in the same historical time and milieu, have not received much
attention. In any event, the term "salon" has lately been challenged, since
it hearkens back rather to French aristocratic customs: restricted gather-
ings in the homes of the nobility featuring artistic performances and
usually accompanied by a lavish meal. Rahel and her peers preferred to
speak of their "open houses," in which they gathered a mixed society
of Jews and Christians, bourgeoisie and nobility, women and men.
The mainstay of this hospitality was conversation.

If never quite a classroom without classes (the demimonde of artists
appeared, but the working class did not), nor a panacea of German Jewish
symbiosis (the Jewish hostesses did not receive return invitations from
their Christian guests), the open houses were nevertheless a space of
intellectual exchange beyond the supervision of rabbinate and university
alike. The removal of the intellectual life of Jews from the traditional
institutions of Jewish learning—synagogue, study house, yeshiva—has
been much remarked, but the extracurricular standing of the open houses
with respect to the university bears emphasizing. Jewish Studies would
find an early welcome in some rabbinical academies, but would remain
on the waiting list for a century before gaining admission to the university
curriculum. Hence, the field would have its first flourishing in voluntary
associations, though, aside from the open houses of Rahel and her cohort,
few non-Jews volunteered to associate. Even now, when it is possible
to earn a degree in Jewish Studies (or Judaic Studies or any number of
variants in nomenclature) in universities throughout the world, such
extracurricular spaces continue to thrive, from major research institutions like the YIVO to the more modest offerings in adult education
sponsored by Jewish community centers. The Jewish Museum in New
York, founded as a collection of ritual objects in the Jewish Theological
Seminary at the turn of the twentieth century, has long since broadened
its purview and offered a public venue for studying Jews, including an
important exhibition in 2005 that considered Rahel and her heirs.[3]

The open houses of late eighteenth- and early nineteenth-century
Berlin are a prototype for Jewish Studies in a related but distinct sense as
well. Reacting against the all but invariable account of the cozy setting of
Rahel's open house, cultural historian Barbara Hahn wonders just how
"a garret on the attic floor of an eighteenth-century house is supposed to
hold some twenty people, along with sofas, a piano, tea tables, and a slew
of chairs."[4] This consideration marks Hahn's formation in the current

state of the question in Jewish Studies, in which material culture has begun to take its place alongside textual study. The perspective allows her to return to the material place of social interaction and from there to contest the political imaginary of prior research projects: "Not much room is left for Jews," she remarks sardonically.[5] She then relocates the scene downstairs, in the living quarters of the whole Levin family, and so reclaims the open house as a Jewish home. Thus, Hahn and scholars of Jewish Studies more generally work against the erasure of Jews. This work, at once political and intellectual, is often carried out as a project of inclusion: where others are, let Jews enter. But the open houses suggest another paradigm. For Rahel was already inside, in the place of hospitality, positioned to extend the invitation.

The shift in the space of the political imaginary from isolated garret to domestic quarters points to a family history, which, in turn, will clarify Rahel's crucial role in constructing the preconditions of Jewish Studies. Rahel's father had already opened his house, attracting not only Jewish kin and friends, but also impecunious Christians currying easy credit. The structural position of Jews in the circulation of money opened one route to modernity for "Shylock's children," especially in the role of "service nomad" assigned to various peoples in various places.[6] But whosoever occupies that economic niche finds it fraught with social peril. The tax farmer who calls for payment is a more immediate target of animosity, for instance, than the ruler who calls for taxation in the first place.

This tendency is strong in the studies of Jews by non-Jews in the milieu and over the long period between the era of Rahel and Arendt. The claim to find an essential, that is, an inherent and ineradicable connection between Jews and money is the crux of the vicious critique of a young Karl Marx in "On the Jewish Question" (1843), for instance, which he only overcame when he enlarged his view to engage capitalism as a system, rather than to castigate its functionaries.

Yet even stripping the discussion of money lending around the table in the Levin household of any antisemitic intention, the gendered structure of commerce touches directly upon the transformation of the open house as it passes from father to daughter. The autobiography of Glückel of Hameln, a German Jewish woman of the late seventeenth and early eighteenth centuries, gives ample evidence that Jewish women were long involved in finance.[7] Nevertheless, the movement of Jews into the newly forming bourgeoisie of German-speaking lands, which begins in the commercial lifetime of the elder Levin, leads to the rapid domestication of women, which is to say to their withdrawal from finance.[8] Rahel's two brothers went into the family business, while she was given tutors in foreign languages, including German, and familiarized herself with their literatures.

Outside of Jewish Studies, Rahel's most secure place lies in literary history. She was not studying Jews; she was studying Wolfgang von Goethe, already renowned from the time of her earliest youth as the author of the sentimental epistolary novel *The Sorrows of Young Werther* (1774). It was Rahel, however, who played the leading role in promoting the Goethe cult, focusing on his later novel *Wilhelm Meister's Apprenticeship* (1795–96). That later work by Goethe provided the chief model of what became, partly through Rahel's activities, a linchpin of modern German culture, namely, the concept of *Bildung* (often translated as self-cultivation), "the knighthood of modernity" combining "the meaning carried by education with character formation."[9] Goethe's Wilhelm seeks by force of education, which here means formative experience rather than classroom study, to achieve the refinement that comes to the nobility effortlessly, as their cultural inheritance. Historian George L. Mosse emphasizes that this path to social ascendancy was especially attractive to Jews, since they were traditionally barred from hereditary titles. The cultural model of self-cultivation became a watchword for Jews of German-speaking lands, and the literary genre of the *Bildungsroman*, exemplified by Goethe's Wilhelm Meister novels, the narrative frame of their collective wish fulfillment.

Goethe makes clear, however, that the attainments of self-cultivation were antithetical to commerce. Wilhelm himself rejects a ready opportunity for commercial success as a dead end. Commerce might lead to leisure, but not to refinement. As a young Jewish woman excluded from her father's commerce, Rahel and other women of her cohort took to the ways of self-cultivation. But since they were not free, like their male model, to wander the countryside in search of edifying experience, they pursued their education through the conversation of the open house.

Arendt discovers that here, too, Goethe proved crucial in that his Wilhelm eschews commerce and chooses instead to go on stage. It is in this performative sense that one may read Arendt's articulation of self-cultivation as Rahel learned it from Goethe: "Wilhelm Meister attempts by acquiring education in the broadest sense to learn to represent himself."[10] Jews both set the stage and acted upon it in the Berlin open houses, *representing themselves* before a mixed society of Jews and their neighbors.

Mortiz Oppenheim, often deemed the first modern Jewish painter, undertook to represent that representation in *Lavater and Lessing Visiting Mendelssohn* of 1856—an object for future Jewish Studies, but also, I propose, already in itself a visual mode of studying Jews in the period immediately following Rahel's era. Oppenheim returns to the earlier cultural moment of the late eighteenth century when he stages a group around a chessboard: in the foreground the Jewish embodiment of the European

Enlightenment, Moses Mendelssohn, sits across the chess table from the Protestant theologian and physiognomist, Johann Caspar Lavater. More than a generalized emblem of the Age of Reason, the match in progress alludes to the play *Nathan the Wise* (1778–79), in which chess has a prominent role. The author of the play, Gotthold Ephraim Lessing, stands behind the table. The chess match also allows the painter to depict the adversarial relationship between the two seated players.

In an open letter of 1769, Lavater had challenged Mendelssohn either to refute Christianity by rational argument or admit the reverse by converting. Lavater's attack facilitates an explication of the difference between a politics of inclusion, commonly the basis of multiculturalism in the current academic curriculum, and a subaltern critique. More often considered in its benign manifestations, inclusion does not necessarily put hegemonic power into question. Lavater invites Mendelssohn to join a discussion, it would seem, and, after all, he would have been only too happy to include him in the Christian fold. For Lavater the goal was a melting-pot understanding of emancipation: emancipating Jews from their Judaism and, ultimately, as Marx bluntly argued, emancipating Europe from its Jews.

It is noteworthy that Lavater calls in rationality as the arbiter. In fact, from Lavater's point of view, rationality stands on the side of Christianity: to speak in a fully rational way is already to be a Christian. For Mendelssohn, to accept debate on these terms is already to lose. To contest the terms and their ramifications, on the other hand, given the real power relations that subtend this and other staged debates between Christians and Jews dating back to the Middle Ages, could only lead to open hostility against him. Oppenheim would mollify the situation. He chooses a moment when "conflict and alliance are held in balance."[11] Moreover, the painter replaces abstract rationality with the concrete historical figure of Mendelssohn's friend Lessing at the very point of balance at the acme of the compositional triangle of the three men. He thus engages an arbiter who may be expected to ensure fair play.

In theory, however, the terms of debate offered by Lavater in order to include Mendelssohn within Christendom were designed to silence him as a Jew. "Can the subaltern speak?" postcolonial theorist and literary critic Gayatri Spivak has asked in our generation.[12] It was already a good question in the successive eras of Mendelssohn, Rahel, and Oppenheim. As Mendelssohn already understood, to answer requires recognition that hegemonic powers reserve for themselves the authority to determine what will count as speech. The subaltern can only speak, therefore, when the terms of debate are overdetermined, undermined, evaded, or otherwise overthrown.

Mendelssohn undertook that political and intellectual task by providing an articulation of Judaism, in lieu of a refutation of Christianity, in his *Jerusalem* (1783). Cultural historian Sander L. Gilman elucidates what might be considered the subaltern resistance of that text accomplished by shifting the debate from theology, Lavater's home field and preferred battleground, to civility. "Mendelssohn's careful answer stresses the need for a sense of decorum in public debate, which cannot take place under such demands [i.e., refute or convert]," writes Gilman. "Indeed, Mendelssohn's defense of Judaism in his *Jerusalem* . . . does not make it into a 'rational' religion, as some later claimed, but into a decorous one."[13] Lavater offers to debate the thesis that it is impossible to be both Jewish and rational. Mendelssohn counters not with an antithesis in Lavater's terms, but with a different mode of speech, illustrating by the example of his own discourse and comportment that it is possible to be both Jewish and decorous. The open houses of Rahel and her cohort were a school for such decorum, and a stage for representing decorous Jews—though the Christian guests often complained in their correspondence that they found their Jewish hosts wanting precisely on this score.

And then comes light refreshment. Oppenheim balances the compositional pyramid of men at the left with a fourth figure, a woman in the doorway to the deeper recesses of the house at the right. Her face shadowed and demurely lowered, she carries a tray: wife or daughter or servant? The difficulty in distinguishing between the alternatives is telling. One registers this implication: if the awkward moment of Lavater's public challenge is to be smoothed away by hospitality, and Mendelssohn himself is to partake, this must be his Jewish home and Mendelssohn the host—as Lessing, Lavater, and Oppenheim would have known full well from Mendelssohn's orthodox practices, which restricted him from eating in non-Jewish houses. But in the following generation, it is the Jewish woman who will step into the light, re-create the institution of the open house, and discover a new Jewish voice.

Arendt listens for that voice. She is in need of it for herself. The philosopher Karl Jaspers, Arendt's mentor and friend, and himself a staunch resister against Heidegger and Nazism, already saw as much when he read the Rahel book in manuscript: "This work still seems to me to be your own working through of the basic questions of Jewish existence, and in it you use Rahel's reality as a guide to help you achieve clarity and liberation for yourself."[14] Jaspers was not trying to steer Arendt away from studying Jews to some other, safer topic; rather he speaks for the canons of scholarly objectivity. Not that Arendt should adopt a more impartial view: on the contrary, Jaspers goes on in the same letter to argue against what he considers to be Arendt's lack of sympathy for a

Rahel "who trembles and bleeds." He writes, "You let this figure speak, but not from her core, that is, not as this human being herself, who is not in her nature a Jew, but who passes through this world as a Jew and therefore experiences the most extreme things, things that happen not only to Jews."[15] Arguing against the essentialism of a Jewish "nature" (i.e., an uneducable, biological imperative), Jaspers finds that Arendt's concentration on Rahel's life as a Jewess limits the humanity of both women, author and subject. In light of the imminent threat of fascism, Jaspers urges that to study Jews as Jews, to insist on the Jewishness of Jews and to emphasize the particularity of a Jewish fate, is to miss the greater and more pressing opportunity to argue for the inclusion of Jews in the more general category of the human. True liberation of each and all, Jew and non-Jew, Arendt and Jaspers, too, would depend upon an effective defense of universal human rights.

Jaspers's humanist position grows out of the legacy of the European Enlightenment, once again dating to the era of Rahel in German-speaking lands—a legacy that engaged Rahel herself. Its anthropology knows of but two poles: the concrete, unique individual and an abstract, undifferentiated humanity. Modern democracy, conceived and dedicated in the same period, grounds political equality on that dual conception of the human. Yet Jaspers's remark about Jews "passing through" the world gives pause. On their way to what other world? Jaspers, it seems, imports a certain theology into his reading of Arendt. And, wherever they may be headed, why are Jews presented as inevitably on the move? Why homeless wanderers (to make explicit the underlying trope of the wandering Jew), when Rahel—and Arendt, for that matter—saw themselves as being quite at home in Germany?

Arendt resisted Jaspers's sympathetic critique as Mendelssohn had resisted its patently malevolent version in Lavater's challenge. A liberal, non-Jewish, German philosopher alarmed by the rise of fascism may pass through Jewishness on the way to human rights and still hope that there will be time to defend Jews within the inclusive category of humanity— 1929 is not 1939. But to adopt such an understanding of Jews, when one is a Jew oneself, Arendt argues, is Rahel's fundamental error, and the mistake from which Arendt would free herself by studying Jews through Rahel's example. Indeed, Arendt's major political thesis in this regard is to posit that Jews were and should have insisted on remaining a corporate entity, and thus to have negotiated their entrance into the modern world as Jews—and, one may infer, their entrance into the modern curriculum as Jewish Studies. Instead, in her view, Jews accepted the advantages of partial freedoms as isolated individuals. Hence, in a different though not unrelated sense to Jaspers's remarks, Arendt claims that Jews attempted to pass, to accept their erasure as Jews as the price of admission to modern Europe. To treat Rahel as a Jewess, a representative case, therefore, is to make a retroactive political argument that Jews failed to make in 1833, a political argument all the more pertinent to Arendt's Germany in 1933. Jaspers characterizes the politics of studying Jews as "liberation for yourself." Against Jaspers, but also against Rahel, Arendt raises the political stakes. The personal is the political in this light. Studying even a single Jew, as long as she is studied as a Jew, makes Jewish Studies function as liberation politics.

Rahel never was given a place at the table, to recall an image from her recurring nightmare, central to Arendt's biography.[16] That Rahel was aware that she remained a Jew, even after she converted and became Varnhagen by marriage, is the cornerstone of Arendt's analysis. That awareness distinguished Rahel from "outright opportunists who always accept the here-and-now, who circumvent unpleasantness with lies and forget the good."[17] This formulation from the opening pages of the biography would later become the Jewish parvenu in Arendt's more widely known essay of 1944, in which the opportunist is counterbalanced by the figure of the pariah, or quintessential outsider, whose recurrence in modern Jewish history constitutes, for Arendt, "a hidden tradition," from which she allows the example of Rahel to vanish.[18]

A telltale sign remains, however, a key word transferred from the life of a Jewess to the career of Rahel's protégé, the German-Jewish poet Heinrich Heine. That key word, which appears already in the title of the first chapter of *Rahel Varnhagen*, is *shlemihl*, the hapless innocent, characterized by Arendt as one "who anticipates nothing."[19] Rahel, for instance, fails to anticipate the rise of German nationalism following Napoleon's invasion, the backlash against the cosmopolitanism of the open houses, the eventual revocation of Jewish emancipation in the areas to which Napoleon had brought the reform from France, and the anti-Jewish riots in Germany in 1819. Needless to say, in these terms, Arendt herself would be an even greater *shlemihl*.

Contemporary literary critic Ruth R. Wisse expands the term in at least two crucial directions. First, while likening the figure to the stock type of the fool in other folk traditions, she underlines the skewed logic of subaltern resistance when she points to the "nonmilitary rather than antimilitary" character of the Jew-in-the-army jokes with which she introduces her study. "It goes without saying," she adds, "that the jokes, structured on a rhythmic counterpoint between two cultures represented by the brusque command or rhetorical challenge and the innocent query, are not as naïve as their subjects."[20] In the native idiom of Yiddish, to represent Jews as *shlemihls* is to cast them as comic fools, of course.

But where brusque command counts as rational discourse and obedience is wisdom, the subaltern may speak after all, but as *shlemihl.*

Furthermore, the inability to anticipate what appears in retrospect as an inevitability is the dimension of fate at the heart of tragedy in classical drama. Wisse argues that the *shlemihl* is not only comic, but also modern. By invoking the *shlemihl* in the understanding of Rahel, therefore, Arendt moves—perhaps despite herself—along the modern bias from fate to history: from a conception of life, particularly Jewish life as the ineluctable replay of an unchanging structure, and hence as ultimately devoid of human agency, to a view of life and of lives oriented around a set of cruxes at which human actors make determinate decisions.

Even so, where the word *shlemihl* comes easily to a scholar of Yiddish literature like Wisse, the term remains a surprise in a text by a middle-class, native German-speaking woman with her recent doctorate in hand circa 1930. In Arendt's social milieu, Yiddish was marked not simply as Jewish but as the language of those too-Jewish Eastern European immigrants whose lack of decorum was such an embarrassment to their more settled Jewish neighbors in New York no less than in Berlin. The later choice of "pariah" links Arendt to the tradition of the founding figures of German social theory, to Max Weber, as Arendt herself notes, and to Georg Simmel, whose study of "the stranger" concludes with the observation that Jews best exemplify that social category.[21] For Arendt to adopt *"shlemihl"* as a key word marks a deliberate effort to return to Jewish sources, to emancipate herself as a Jew, to speak as the subaltern, who will often adopt the trickster's reversal of naming oneself with just those tags used by others to assert marginalization.

Arendt returns no farther back than Rahel. As noted, she did not take into her account of Jewish fate or Jewish history the many Jews over many centuries who did indeed anticipate something, the coming of the Messiah, nor the prophets, who anticipated everything. She ignored the century of scholarship in Jewish Studies that grew up between her and Rahel that might have taught her a wider range of terms than opportunist and *shlemihl*, parvenu and pariah. And she further removed herself from Jewish Studies and most Jewish communities by her controversial reportage on the trial of Adolf Eichmann, a chief Holocaust perpetrator, and, to a lesser extent, by her unquestioning postwar public commitment to Heidegger, despite what Holocaust scholar Berel Lang has characterized as "Heidegger's Silence" with respect to his involvement with the Nazis.[22] Hence, while her status in political philosophy has never been in question, her place in Jewish Studies has only lately begun to be rehabilitated, even in Jerusalem.[23]

The vicissitudes of Arendt's career notwithstanding, her meeting with Rahel provides an exemplary tale for the formation of the terms of debate in Jewish Studies in several regards. First, where Jewish learning stakes its authority to antiquity by dint of a claim to an unbroken tradition reaching back to Sinai, Jewish Studies is predicated upon the conceptualization of significant breaks that always mark a relative modernity. In seeking out a precedent in Rahel for her own break with Jewish tradition, Arendt paradoxically demonstrates through that precedent that the break never fully took place for either of them—Jews are *shlemihls* even when it comes to distancing themselves from things Jewish. In so doing, Arendt makes a case vital for Jewish Studies, namely, that Jewish modernity, however conceived and historically situated, can be taken as a Jewish source, and not only as a falling away from the sources. The general proposition is all the more important for Jewish women, as both subject and object of Jewish Studies, since in antiquity, again however conceived and already at Sinai, Jewish women were put under erasure.

Second, Arendt makes a more pointed argument in the conception of modernity that she develops by studying Rahel. She depicts Rahel not only as particularly Jewish, as opposed to the Enlightenment ideal of the universally human, but also as a strikingly early Jewish example of the modern self, to use philosopher Charles Taylor's term.[24] In Arendt's account, Rahel is already a person endowed with agency (author of her own desires and intentions, and capable of realizing them by her own efforts) and also riven by a fissure between an unchanging and authentic interior and a mobile, performative exterior. That it is possible to be both a Jew and a self has proven to be a more enduring thesis than Mendelssohn's related argument that it is possible to be both Jewish and decorous. And it is that Jew as modern self, more choosing than chosen, that provides the crucial precondition for Jewish Studies as it emerged in the subsequent decades of the nineteenth century—much as the open house offers something of a prototype for its institutional space. For Jewish learning is the fulfillment of a covenantal obligation, while studying Jews is an academic choice.

## Jewish Science

German Jewish thinker Moses Hess could barely sell his *Rome and Jerusalem: The Last Nationalist Question* when it appeared in 1862, but whom did he expect to buy it? His once influential socialist vision had been repudiated by his erstwhile colleagues, Marx and Engels, and their alternative insistence on class as a social factor drew an international map for radical politics. In the wake of the *Communist Manifesto* (1843), nationalism would indeed have been just about the last question on the minds of the radical left. Christian readers who were led by the reference in the title to Rome *and* Jerusalem to expect a cheerful program of rapprochement with Jews, or at least decorous debate, would have been taken aback by the pugnacious imputations of "Christian hostility to culture" in the past and "Christian German Anti-Semitism" in the present from the very first page of the author's preface.[25] Among Jews, the German language of the text in itself would have been a barrier to those dedicated to traditional Jewish learning. And the moderns, divided among themselves by the conflict between the new Reform movement then gaining strength in German-speaking lands and the neo-Orthodox reaction to it, would have found Hess's most consistent polemic directed against both parties. The publisher would have found one further obstacle: no course adoption policy. The recent petition of Rabbi Abraham Geiger, the leading intellectual figure of the Reform movement, to include Jewish Studies in the Faculty of Theology in a German university had been rejected. Jewish Studies would remain an extracurricular activity for some time to come.

If Hess was to have a reader for his ideas, he would have to invent her. And he did. The book is structured as one side of a correspondence, written by a patently autobiographical persona, which allows Hess to imagine the addressee of the letters and occasionally to allude to her reactions. The portrait of Hess's ideal reader may be pieced together from a few details about this unnamed fictional addressee (the real-life model was his sister-in-law to be). She is a young woman not only well acquainted with the Bible, but also "well-versed in the higher philosophical conceptions of German thought."[26] She seems at least somewhat inclined toward the Reform movement, since the letter writer chides her for her assumption that "only our progressive Jews [i.e., Reform Jews] have acquired the mastery of modern culture and science and that orthodox Jews are still steeped in Egyptian darkness."[27] Finally, she appears to have reservations about Hess's thinking. Only after half of the correspondence has been completed does the letter writer declare, "You have finally begun to interest yourself in Jewish affairs"[28]—an ideal reader indeed, if she has been so patient.

A different patience eventually gains another crucial reader for Hess's *Rome and Jerusalem* in Theodor Herzl, the journalist turned political organizer, who gathered various Jewish nationalist questions into an international Zionist movement. Herzl came across the obscure book by chance and retroactively recognized Hess's colonial project for settling Jews as agents of European powers in economically strategic locations in the Middle East as a precursor to his own more radical plan to create an independent Jewish State. Here, as in many other ways, Herzl has cast the decisive vote, and Hess's place in Jewish Studies is generally circumscribed to the role of a proto-Zionist. The want of a key word, "Zionism," to focus the disparate interests and positions articulated in *Rome and Jerusalem* may be taken as an additional explanation as to why the text could find no apt readership among Hess's contemporaries.

Scholar of religion Ken Koltun-Fromm has argued against those who see *Rome and Jerusalem* as diffuse, if not to say simply confused, by emphasizing its epistolary form. The convention of the open letter had been raised to a leading genre in eighteenth-century fictional and didactic works. Rahel insisted, for instance, that her addressees share what we might otherwise call her private letters with other friends. The open letter created a supplementary space overlapping and intermixing private and public domains; it was a textual form of the open house, a space for representing oneself in the deliberately ambiguous sense of both donning a mask and yet allowing a glimpse of the face. The letter writer's (and Hess's) desultory autobiographical narrative embedded in the text may appear at odds with Hess's philosophical purposes. But the relation of "conversionary experiences"[29] accounts for shifts in his positions as the trajectory of his own self-cultivation. The most important of these was the impact of the internationally publicized blood-libel trial in Damascus in 1840, in which Jews were accused of murdering monks for the purpose of using their blood in connection with Passover rites. The event both shocked and mobilized Jews throughout the world, and led Hess to begin to take an interest in Jewish affairs. Through his letter writer, Hess offers the results of the unorthodox cultivation of his Jewish self as the basis for the extracurricular course in Jewish Studies for his unnamed addressee.

The letter writer's apprenticeship includes a political career that orients his approach to studying Jews. The text speaks of the conversionary experience of a sojourn in France for a native of autocratic Prussia: "Springtime in the life of nations began with the French Revolution," he exclaims.[30] The enthusiasm for democracy on the part of the letter writer occludes the commitment to socialism of Hess, the author, who only came to France as an exile as a result of his socialist activities. In this light the significant break in the education of the author, which the letter writer connects to the defeat of a popular uprising in Prussia, rather than the rejection of Hess by Marx and Engels, is the moment when "I withdrew from politics and devoted myself entirely to natural sciences."[31]

Koltun-Fromm reconstructs an underlying unity in *Rome and Jerusalem* by subsuming its internal differences under the heading of identity, a term central to the current state of Jewish Studies. Hess, on the other hand, speaks the language of his times when he organizes his approach to studying Jews around the term "science." The Berlin open houses, once again, offer an introduction. The first of these was the open house of Markus and Henrietta Herz. Markus had studied medicine at the university, an important entryway for Jewish men into modern European life at a time when almost all other university studies were closed to them. But he took advantage of his stay in Koenigsburg to attend the lectures of Immanuel Kant and thus to study the new critical philosophy at the source. When Markus returned to Berlin he married Henrietta, more than twenty years his junior, and began to give lectures and demonstrations in their home in the natural sciences, drawing much of his audience from the mixed Jewish and non-Jewish clientele of his successful medical practice. Henrietta soon opened a parallel session in a different room, dedicated to her interests in languages and literatures, which was the immediate precursor to Rahel's still more influential open house. When Henrietta wrote in her memoir, "I attracted [people] through my beauty and through the understanding I had for all kinds of *sciences,*" the word she used was "Wissenschaften," which was indeed broad enough to include the interests of both husband and wife, developed against the backdrop of a Kantian understanding of critical scholarship.[32]

When Hess declares in the preface of *Rome and Jerusalem* that "the field of Jewish science is common to reformers and the orthodox alike,"[33] he expresses that broad understanding of science and also constitutes an open allusion to the intellectual movement known as the *Wissenschaft des Judentums,* usually translated as The Science of Judaism. The expression derived from the name that a group of young Jewish men gave to their small, voluntary Society for the Culture and Science of the Jews, and more precisely from the title of the related journal for studying Jews. The Wissenschaft movement is generally taken as the inauguration of modern Jewish Studies.

To study Jews scientifically, as critical scholars, meant to study Jews historically. In this, the Wissenschaft scholars worked within the intellectual presuppositions and methodologies that they had learned from the conduct of other fields in German universities. The German linguist Wilhelm von Humboldt, a frequenter of Rahel's open house, and eventually the architect of the curriculum of the modern German university, articulated "The Task of the Historian" in a lecture by that title delivered to the Prussian Academy of Sciences in 1821. "One has . . . scarcely arrived at the skeleton of an event by a crude sorting out of what actually happened. . . . To stop here would be to sacrifice the actual inner truth. . . . The truth of any event is predicated on the addition . . . of that invisible part of every fact, and it is this part, therefore, which the historian has to add."[34] "What actually happened" became a motto for the mode of research, often referred to as historicism, that dominated much of the nineteenth century; "the actual inner truth," however, is the fulcrum for transformation of Jewish learning into the new, scientific Jewish Studies.

One may discern the process of metaphorization in a programmatic statement by Isaac Marcus Jost, a member of the original Society for the Science and Culture of the Jews, and the author of the *General History of the Jewish People* (1832), the first comprehensive historiographical work in the Wissenschaft movement. In "Rigors of Jewish Historiography," an introduction to his later, condensed compendium of that work, Jost makes the following distinction:

> Theology solves questions which history does not pose or must leave unanswered. If it derives data from history, it seeks not merely to disclose in them the causes and effects suggested by historical research, but rather the revelations of divine judgment and divine providence.
>
> History, on the other hand, limits itself to representing what has occurred in accordance with the causes which disclose themselves to the observant eye and with the consequences that develop from them according to the laws of nature.[35]

The issue is epistemological, though the implications are ethical. Jost would circumscribe the limits of what may be known within the purview of history, while admitting that there is more to heaven and earth. Nevertheless, diligent historical research will push back the limits, expanding the scope of human agency, and hence human responsibility. It is by such means that the cause of liberty is furthered. Daring to know what can be known frees humankind from the fetters of its self-incurred minority, Kant had declared in his famous response to the question, "What is enlightenment?" (1784).[36] The epistemological and methodological model for that daring, Jost suggests, is the investigation of "the laws of nature," which is to say that he links the discipline of modern, critical history to the sciences, now more narrowly understood.

Yet Humboldt's "invisible part" would not be accessible to even the most "observant eye." The historian's task is not merely data collecting; it requires a hermeneutic method as well. The "inner truth" of history is arrived at by interpretation, if not to say, as Humboldt does boldly, that it is added onto the facts. For Jost, the hermeneutical model is clear: the exegetical approach of Jewish learning to the Hebrew Scriptures. The point requires careful delineation, since an alternative exegetical program was readily available and in fact formed part of the immediate intellectual background of the Wissenschaft movement.

Christian Hebraists have regularly applied historical methods to the reading of the Hebrew Scriptures since the eighteenth century, and one result of their philological research is the thesis of the multi-strand composition of the Bible, still very much the scholarly norm today.[37] The argument for separate, multiple authorships redacted at a late date relative to the first textual traditions was fueled by a perception of imperfections in the editing of the final form: redundancy, non-sequiturs, internal contradictions, and so on. The exegetical presupposition, therefore, was that sense is achieved by a smoothly articulated narrative line; conversely, any form of textual disruption would be nonsense. Since nonsense could not be attributed to God, the Hebrew Scriptures must be the work of human hands, subject to the philological vicissitudes of textual transmission over a long history.

Rabbinical exegesis concedes that the Torah is written in human language, which makes it accessible to human readers, but at the same time obscures more-than-human meaning. What are errors from the point of view of the Christian Hebraists are invitations to interpretation for the rabbis. The linear forward motion of the narrative drive of Hebrew Scriptures guides one level of reading. But then there is the hermeneutic overdrive that leads rabbinic readers back and forth, ranging over the whole text without regard for chronological order or narrative sequence in search of connections that will bring to light the overdetermined meanings that saturate every detail. Jost expounds the principle: "In every book, in every paragraph—one is tempted to say in every expression— one sees the entire spirit of the people with its traditions and its relationships, a complete world."[38] But inasmuch as the record of creation is also the blueprint of the laws of nature, according to Jewish learning, the world itself is organized like the text and susceptible to the same hermeneutic approach. Thus, Jost writes that the "inner unity is its truth for the historian."[39]

The historical method of the Science of Judaism may well depart from Jewish learning inasmuch as it splits off the domain of human agency as the object of its research, leaving the question of God's will to the concerns of theology. But the Wissenschaft movement still imports the ground concept of inner unity as its truth and invisible part from the Jewish reading of the Bible. Jewish history is, metaphorically, the Scripture of Jewish science.

The chief historian of nineteenth-century Jewish Studies, Heinrich Graetz, does not hesitate to give that inner unity a name in another programmatic statement that he published prior to his own comprehensive, multivolume *History of the Jews from Earliest Times to the Present* (1853–1875).[40] In his oft-cited essay, "The Structure of Jewish History," Graetz explains that scholars bring the multiplicity of facts concerning Jewish texts and Jewish acts to light, but, as "these facts can be used to show that Jewish history in all its phases, even in the apparent aberrations of the moment, exhibits a single idea, that in fact, it constitutes a concrete explication of a fundamental concept."[41] For Graetz, that idea may be stated simply: "The concept of God must immediately become a concept of the state."[42] The concept of God is patent, even where Jews lived with little or no political autonomy, so it is the concept of the state that was the invisible part of Jewish history in many periods. It was the concept of the state that must immediately be made manifest in studying Jews critically, scientifically, historically. Thus, Graetz opens volume 1 of his *History of the Jews* not with the foundations of monotheism in the period of the biblical patriarchs (to which he circles back a few pages later), but with the dawning of the ancient state: "It was on a spring day that some pastoral tribes passed across the Jordan into a strip of land which can only be regarded as an extended coast-line of the Mediterranean. This was the land of *Canaan*, subsequently called *Palestine*."[43]

Graetz's "single idea" was also manifested in Hess's fundamental concept of soil, in *Rome and Jerusalem*. The shift in scientific register from Graetz's history to Hess's natural sciences is idiosyncratic, and Hess, at most, is but a minor figure in the Wissenschaft movement. But working in the quite different context of the relationship between modern Hebrew and Yiddish literature and other literary modernisms, Chana Kronfeld urges a strategic reversal that is cogent for this case as well: "Construct the major through the minor, not—as current wisdom has it—the minor through the major."[44] Hess, like Rahel, can be dismissed as incidental to the Wissenschaft movement and Jewish Studies, an amateur historian unable to achieve in his muddled way what Jost and better yet Graetz accomplished with a fully elaborated historical method. Alternatively, reading the Wissenschaft movement through Hess, and the turn to history through his recourse to botany, will shed light on the stakes of studying Jews as a science. First of all, the strategy helps to reveal the way in which the reduction of the diversity of Jewish experience to the operant factor of Jost's "inner unity" or Graetz's "single idea" has created hierarchies within Jewish Studies analogous to those in which Jewish Studies is subordinated to other "standard" fields. To treat Hess as pre-Herzl, like Christian readings of the so-called Old Testament prefigurations that are superseded and fulfilled in the New, is to miss the opportunity to understand Hess as being already Hess.

Hess's natural science of Jewishness is a political project. Its first aim is to reconstruct Jewish difference among the nations as a form of equality. The self-evident purpose of such parity is a defense against Christian hostility, which reduces Jewish difference to prefiguration: pre-Christian, not yet fully civilized, susceptible of "civic improvement" at best, as Mendelssohn's Christian friend Dohm argued, if not inherently depraved.

But Hess in fact wastes little time debating the Lavaters and Dohms of his period, even if the Damascus Affair alerted him to a recrudescent anti-Jewish sentiment. Instead, his botanism, so to speak, is an anti-humanism, insofar as the humanistic vision can recognize only individual human agents and universal human rights and thus, as Hahn said, leave little room for Jews. "Just as Nature does not produce flowers and fruits of a general character," writes Hess in the ninth letter, "nor general plants and animal types, so does the creative power in history produce only folk types."[45] It will be necessary to return to the implications of the passing reference to a "creative power in history," which imports an underdetermined, deistic note into the discussion. Attending to the main argument for now, Hess recognizes that species may be grouped under more generic classifications for the purposes of the organization of knowledge, but emphasizes that as they exist in nature, the species remain distinct. The same taxonomic system significantly qualifies the autonomy of the self as the locus of agency, while allowing for change over time and ontological continuity. The acorn is not free to become a rose, but neither is it an oak until it grows into a tree.

Evil enters the botanical garden not through the fact of differentiation, but through the fiction of racial superiority. Jews are a race and Germans are a race, in Hess's account; the problem facing Jews in Germany is that "the Teutomaniac, in his love of the Fatherland, loves not the State but the race dominance."[46] Needless to say, the discourse of race is deployed in the nineteenth and twentieth centuries with increasing ferocity as a pseudo-scientific justification for mythologies of "race dominance." And studying Jews as a race within Jewish Studies abets the racialization of Jews in modern antisemitism, especially where, as in Hess's case, the biological model is vitiated by the absence of a concept of cross-fertilization and the implications of hybridity.

Hess's second political aim is articulated through an environmental paradigm. As historians in his adopted home in nineteenth-century France were already beginning to argue, and their heirs in the twentieth-century French *Annales* School of historians would develop in a different way, Hess links his notion of folk-types to concrete habitats. The predominant idiom of the text in this regard, as in others, is botanical: certain plants are native to certain soils, which represent a necessary condition for flourishing. This environmental consideration is inflected along the lines of Hess's "true socialism." To say that a people separated from its native soil can only live by attaching itself to other folk who are rooted, and thus that such a people has "the status of a parasite,"[47] is to explicate a natural science metaphor in common parlance as an antisemitic slur, a near neighbor to the epithet of Jewish vermin. Hess gives the figure a further, economic twist, when he recasts the separation of Jews from the soil to mean that in their niche as service nomads they are constrained to unproductive labor. True socialism would require that Jews become productive, which means above all for both Hess and, later, many forms of Zionism to till the soil.

Neither of these political arguments leads to a proposal to resettle in the ancestral territory of the biblical promise. After many centuries in German-speaking lands, for instance, Jews might have made a claim that they were already living on native soil; and political and economic reforms might have made agricultural production more accessible to them. That Hess should close *Rome and Jerusalem* by outlining his colonial project in which, after all, Jews would become commercial agents, not farmers, cannot be accounted for as a logical consequence of his argument.

Instead of the predominant natural science model, "the trope of 'return'"[48] is Hess's literary device through which he speaks in an alternative register. The literary dimension of Hess's text is not opposed to the scientific in the form of antithesis or contradiction. Rather the two idioms are mixed—a hybrid text—in such a way as to put into question the split that the Wissenschaft movement sought to work between theology and history, or more broadly between the domain of religion and the secular, always in favor of secularization as an expansion of human agency. The division was already qualified by the metaphorization of rabbinic hermeneutics, as seen in Jost's work, in the Wissenschaft conception of the task of the historian. Here, the language of "the creative power in history" noted above is consonant with a variety of explicit references to the philosopher Baruch Spinoza of the seventeenth-century Sephardic community of Amsterdam, which serve to underwrite the hybrid ascription "theo-political" (from the title of one of Spinoza's chief works) to Hess's *Rome and Jerusalem*.

In order to capture Hess's reversal of a reversal—from secularization to theo-politics—it is necessary once again to read the major through the minor. One must read the natural science paradigm for a political argument based on historical analysis through the submerged and intermittent autobiographical narrative. Moreover, one must read the didactic text addressed to the unnamed woman through her absent letters, through the lessons that she would teach her teacher. As her religious instruction is unorthodox, it may be best illuminated by allowing the major to speak first for itself.

Still marginal, as a Jewish text in a Christian culture, but at or near the top of the margin (the category of the subaltern demands finer distinctions), Rabbi Samson Raphael Hirsch's *Nineteen Letters* (1836) was something of a best seller. A didactic work in epistolary form, the *Nineteen*

*Letters* articulated and disseminated the doctrines of the new Orthodoxy. Hess, for one, was familiar with it and refers to the book explicitly. Hirsch's fictional correspondence is two-sided. Like Hess's unnamed woman, Hirsch's Benjamin is a young person pursuing "the mastery of modern culture and science" in nineteenth-century Germany. Looking ahead to his approaching marriage, however, Benjamin finds that his education has not prepared him to meet the responsibilities of a Jewish man in a Jewish home: "When I think of the duties of fatherhood that might possibly devolve on me," he writes in the first letter in the volume, "I tremble."[49] Benjamin's trembling, and fear, one might say, constitute a spiritual crisis, nowhere apparent in the female addressee of the letters of *Rome and Jerusalem*.

Benjamin seeks the counsel of his friend Naphtali, a rabbi who has also read European literature and philosophy, like Hirsch himself, and yet propounds a neo-Orthodox doctrine. Naphtali responds by transmitting passages from the Hebrew Scriptures in Hirsch's German translation—despite his initial insistence that "we must read the Torah in *Hebrew*"[50]—couched in more limited references to rabbinic tradition and Naphtali's own commentaries. Like *Rome and Jerusalem*, then, the *Nineteen Letters* is an introductory course for readers who are no longer acquainted with the fundamentals of Jewish learning. Gender difference will prove a self-conscious issue for Hess, but at the outset his unnamed woman and Benjamin are on par in one specific regard, for Jewish learning is itself gendered male, and in his ignorance Benjamin is "a man who is like a woman."[51]

The *Nineteen Letters* frame the tensions of Jewish modernity as a matter of Jewish religious practice. Thus, Hirsch accepts the terms of debate offered by Lavater in his match with Mendelssohn. Against Hirsch's liberal adversaries, Naphtali argues that "we Jews need to be reformed through Judaism," and not the reverse, reforming Judaism to fit the lives of contemporary Jews.[52] But under the influence of Reform, Naphtali also argues against an older orthodoxy, for which "study became the end instead of the means."[53] He adds with some vehemence, "That method, however, is not truly Jewish. Our great masters have always protested against . . . this false and perverted procedure"; and he cites the adage, "To learn and to teach, to observe and to do."[54]

Hess might well subscribe. As a form of teaching, *Rome and Jerusalem* is a plan of action. But he differs radically from Hirsch in that the practices that he would have his student learn are plainly political. This, too, would be a debate in Lavater's terms, arguing for political emancipation at the price of accepting the silencing of Jewish voices in the domain of theology or even erasing Jews as Jews. For once he separates himself from revolutionary politics, what will prevent a Jew like Hess from returning to Germany as his native soil, and putting his botanical studies at the service of agricultural production? Would Hess himself, married to a non-Jew, at a time when the mother's Jewishness was definitive, have trembled before the demands of raising Jewish children?

And yet from the very first line to his female addressee, Hess's letter writer charts the trope of return as a Jewish move: "After an estrangement of twenty years, I am back with my people."[55] Hess's return may well represent *the* Jewish move in modernity, though variously enacted and articulated. Return constitutes both their Jewishness and their modernity. Reading Hess through the Wissenschaft program makes him a digression along the path of secularization that leads away from Jewish learning as a premodern condition. Reading Wissenschaft scholarship and its avatars through Hess brings to the fore the manner in which Jewish Studies is also conducted along the disparate paths of a return.

The modern attainment of Jewishness is predicated upon an experience of loss—the loss of Jewish learning on the part of Hirsch's Benjamin is exemplary. For Hess, and his letter writer, return to the Jewish people requires a model for an attachment that can sustain itself in the face of loss. "Is it mere chance, that whenever I stand at a new turn in my life, there appears in my path an unhappy woman, who imparts to me daring and courage to travel the unknown road?" he asks.[56] But the question is rhetorical because "every Jewess"[57] is his potential teacher of a melancholia that resists the modern impulse to historicize, that is, to complete what Freud called the work of mourning by consigning the dead to the past and rewarding the living with the present. The gendered instruction, as he sees it, opens the unknown road of return by initiating him into a botanical language beyond the ken of science.

Return to Germany, Hess's letter writer relates, made possible the return to the Jewish cemetery where his parents were buried. "I had forgotten the prayer usually read by Jews over the graves of their departed, and in ignorance my lips murmured the passage from the second of the eighteen benedictions: 'Thou, O Lord, art mighty forever, thou restorest the dead to life,'" he writes to his unnamed addressee. His ignorance, clearly, is not total; and one might say that even had he known no words of prayer at all, awareness that there were words, unknown to him and others, appropriate to a Jewish cemetery, would still have sufficed to mark his path as a return. He is engaged in his makeshift prayer, "when suddenly I noticed a lone flower on a nearby grave. Mechanically I picked it, carried it home with me and put it among my papers." The trope of the soil enters the text on that literal ground. He then closes the anecdote: "Only later, I learned whose earthly remains rest beneath that mound.

I knew then that the treasure, as you named the flower, belongs to you alone." One may read a sublimated eroticism in his picking of the treasure of her flower, but that would be consistent with his own understanding of the scene of instruction as a lesson in mystical union—not between himself and his female correspondent, but rather the "mystic relations between the living and the dead."[58] And these mystic relations fuse with his historical analysis and liberation project to form Hess's mode of studying Jews theo-politically.

Hess's contention, "Oh, how stupid are those who minimize the value of woman's influence upon the development of Judaism,"[59] is no more a straightforward prototype of contemporary feminism than his recourse to natural science is a simple precursor to a political science articulation of contemporary Zionism. And when he describes the melancholic Jewish woman as a "Mater Dolorosa,"[60] he gives evidence of his formation within a hegemonic Christian culture and his relative ignorance of traditional Jewish learning, mitigated by a subsequent reference to "the voice of Rachel, weeping at the fate of her unhappy children" as presented in the Book of Jeremiah.[61] The minor, mystic strain of *Rome and Jerusalem*, too, is closer to Goethe's "elective affinities" than to kabbalistic sources. Nevertheless, this mysticism, crucial to Hess's Jewish turn and return, sounds a hushed note that will later reverberate in Gershom Scholem's work on the Kabbalah, which comes to be exemplary of Jewish Studies as it enters the period that may be called its current state.

Scholem was a contemporary and friend of Arendt, at least until the controversy over her *Eichmann in Jerusalem*, about which they had an acrimonious exchange.[62] Along with her and Rosenzweig, discussed briefly in the preface, Scholem may be taken to frame the end of the inaugural period in the formation of Jewish Studies and its terms of debate. The epochal moment is especially clear, and the date especially significant, in Scholem's critique of the Wissenschaft movement in his "introduction to a lecture which will not take place" in Jerusalem in 1944.[63]

According to Scholem, Jewish Studies as practiced in nineteenth-century Germany failed, utterly, due to an inability to grapple with a set of inner contradictions. Scholem's list reads as follows: (1) the contradiction between the professions of "a pure and objective science" and "the political function which this discipline was intended to fulfill"; (2) the contradiction between their mixed sources in the Enlightenment and in Romanticism, that is "rationalistic evaluations" on the one hand and "the elevation of the aura and brilliance attached to the past by virtue of its being the past," on the other; and (3) "the central contradiction in this entire great adventure called the Science of Judaism: that the conservative tendencies and destructive tendencies within this discipline are interwoven with one another."[64]

The thrust of the first point touches directly upon science as a key word in Jewish Studies. However, broadly conceived, the epistemological aim of science, reaching back at least to the mathematician-philosopher Descartes, called for the circumscribing of the field of research to a domain in which certainty was possible. In the realm of science, dogma was merely received opinion, and opinion, whether received or invented anew, was to be set aside in favor of objectivity. As was clear to the generation of Arendt and Scholem, Jewish Studies was a form of liberation politics—though this was also already true for Graetz, no less than Hess— whose edge was blunted by the pretense to objectivity.

The antiquarian interests of a certain historicism, stockpiling facts of all sorts, is the major target of Scholem's second critique, but it also serves to distinguish his goals and working methods even from the marginal, hybrid text of Hess. The rationalist discourse of the natural sciences, which Scholem associates with the Enlightenment, intersects with the enthusiasm of the Romantic reaction precisely in Hess's botanical idiom, which was at once the source of an orderly taxonomy of nations and of a mystic language of flowers. Despite the dynamism made available through the metaphors of the birth and death, growth and decay of nations, Scholem detects a fundamental conservatism. The organic paradigm imports an essentialism—a biological core, rather than a historical construction—to studying Jews, most nefariously in the conception of Jews as a race. And is a racial conception good for the Jews? It may be recalled that where Hirsch's Naphtali would help his Benjamin to transmit an attenuated Jewish learning forward to his future children, Hess's letter writer is incited to Jewish Studies by the model of the unnamed woman's attachment to the past in the form of her memorial to her dead parents. And as a Zionist in 1944, Scholem was still looking forward to the as yet unfulfilled project of an independent Jewish state; indeed that future, rather than an endless mourning for the countless dead, was the Zionist memorial.

Scholem explicates the third contradiction, more properly the dialectical relationship, between conservative and destructive tendencies in Jewish Studies by recounting an altogether different practice of graveside observance than Hess's memorialization. Jewish historians, now in the guise of giants, now as midgets, dig graves for the particularities of Jewish life and cover them with dry grasses: "The embalmed facts are spread out in the graves, line after line, marked by plot number, as if they were not merely notes. The monuments which are upon the graves, the text, is also so to speak sunken into the earth, and the letters have become faint and the language rubbed out," Scholem relates.[65] Such was the state of the question until two "truly demonic figures" break into the scene: the historian Leopold Zunz, who laid out an enduring research agenda still discernible in much Jewish Studies scholarship in the present day, and the bibliographer Moritz Steinscheider.

Zunz and Steinscheider are major figures in the Wissenschaft movement, whom Scholem would read against the grain of their understanding of science. Zunz's "On Rabbinic Literature" (1818) was an inaugural text for the movement and it proved an outline of Jewish Studies up to the challenge of Scholem, Arendt, and Rosenzweig. Zunz's program was an editorial salvage mission. Although already suffering the effects of neglect, Zunz nevertheless predicted that "Hebrew books are more readily available than they will likely be in 1919."[66] Adjusting his prediction by two decades to account for Nazi book burning, the eerie prescience of the remark has long been noted. Nevertheless, the immediate sequel in Zunz's understanding, namely, that "no new significant development is likely to disturb our survey [of extant literature],"[67] proved to be an underestimation of the materials to be retrieved and the persistence of researchers in his scientific mode over the course of the subsequent century. To cite, first, a transformative instance at an oblique angle to Zunz's exclusive focus on books, archaeological excavation at Dura-Europas in 1932–33 uncovered abundant figural representations in synagogue frescoes, thereby challenging centuries of understanding of the Decalogue prohibition concerning image making. C. H. Kraeling already declares in the initial publication of the archeological survey, "Until quite recently it was generally supposed that ancient Judaism had no art worthy of the name," that is until turn-of-the-century studies of medieval illuminated Jewish manuscripts. The Dura-Europas frescos not only support an alternative assessment of Jewish art history, but also "speak eloquently about Jewish life and thought."[68] The recovery of material culture and correlated life practices, in other words, has indeed contributed to a more variegated view than the elite bases of the Science of Judaism had allowed.

And then there are also Jewish books that have come to disturb the hegemony of rabbinic literature in Zunz's program, most spectacularly the findings at Qumran, in what was still the Land and not yet the State of Israel in 1947. Here, too, the corresponding scholarship was not contained within the precinct of the university, but rather carried over to publications by commercial presses. Yet even that popularizing venue bears witness to the reconstruction offered by contemporary Qumran scholar Lawrence H. Schiffman, in a review of the history of research into the Dead Sea Scrolls.[69] Schiffman rehearses a story that recalls both the philological investigations of Christian Hebraism into the textual sources of the Hebrew Scriptures, as well as the general orientation of biblical archaeology in Ottoman Palestine. For as long as Christian scholars of the

American School of Oriental Research and the French École Biblique and other allied institutions retained a literal monopoly over the scrolls, the contents were almost always presented so as to shed light primarily on the formative period of Christianity. Only when scholars of Jewish Studies were able to break that monopoly and gain direct access to the texts did it become apparent that the Qumran community was a Jewish sect and that studying the Dead Sea Scrolls meant studying Jews. Once again, a political question of who is guest and who is host: Schiffman characterized the change as "Liberating the Scrolls."

Emerging at another angle from Zunz's editorial project, Jewish science liberated the scrolls from rabbinic authority, by reorganizing the canonical texts of Jewish learning. In what was still czarist Russia, for instance, in the years immediately following the bloody pogrom at Kishinev in 1903 that would inspire his poems "On the Slaughter" and "In the City of Slaughter," Chaim Nachman Bialik collaborated with journalist and publisher Yehoshua Hana Ravnitsky in the compilation of *The Book of Legends*, which brought together *aggadic* (i.e., narrative, rather than prescriptive) materials from classical Jewish sources.[70] Bialik and Ravnitsky presented this material in generally continuous narrative sequences in chronological order for nearly half its pages before branching off through a variety of topics that might generally be housed under the rubric of religious concepts and practices. Yet introducing *The Book of Legends*, a contemporary scholar of Midrash, David Stern emphasizes that Aggadah is a traditional theoretical category for texts that exist rather in a state of dispersion in at least three senses. First, Aggadah is "an almost entirely unsystematized, unorganized body of materials of truly bewildering variety," Stern notes. Second, aggadic texts were "typically not preserved as generically independent or self-standing material," but rather "typically appear within the context of a more complex literary form or in the course of a lengthier, extended discussion." And finally, wherever they appear, *Aggadoth* are "recorded in a style that is typically fragmentary and elusive."[71] Bialik and Ravnitsky, therefore, work against the grain of traditional Aggadah in their editorial work, creating a relatively systematic, purely aggadic body of texts in a readable format.

The force of the editorial reorganization may be measured against an aggadic tradition related to the exegesis of Proverbs 15:23, "How good is a word rightly timed," that Bialik and Ravnitsky include under the heading of "Torah" in *The Book of Legends*. Drawing on a talmudic text (B. Sanhedrin 101a), they relate: "Our masters taught: He who recites a verse from Song of Songs and treats it as a secular air [disregarding the traditional cantillation] or he who during a meal recites a verse out of the context where it belongs [for no purpose other than to entertain] brings evil upon the world." The teaching is then amplified with a narrative coda: "Because our Torah girds itself in sackcloth, stands before the Holy One, says, Master of the universe, Your children have turned me into a harp to be played by frivolous people."[72] What shall Torah say before Bialik and Ravnitsky's excavations and recontextualization? They move beyond the project of scientific preservation to a process of editorial reconstruction. And in his massively erudite *The Legends of the Jews* (1909–1938), Lithuanian-born rabbi Louis Ginzberg goes even farther in this direction under the American auspices of the recently established Jewish Publication Society in Philadelphia.[73] A preeminent figure in the American Conservative movement from his faculty position at the Jewish Theological Seminary and the first professor of halakhah at the Hebrew University of Jerusalem, Ginzberg not only adds non-Jewish sources to his multivolume compendium reorganizing rabbinic literature as folklore, but also homogenizes the disparate voices and fragmentary presentation of his material in his own authorial retelling. Like Bialik and Ravnitsky, Ginzberg has moved beyond Zunz's science.

The *Legends of the Jews* follows immediately upon Ginzberg's participation in *The Jewish Encyclopedia: A Descriptive Record of the History, Religion, Literature, and Customs of the Jewish People from the Earliest Times to the Present Day* (1901–1906), under the direction of Cyrus Adler, who had taught Semitics at Johns Hopkins University toward the end of the nineteenth century and would go on to become the founder and president of the American Jewish Historical Society in 1892 and, still later, president of the Jewish Theological Seminary in the early twentieth century. Adler's career path is telling for what it omits: no program wholly dedicated to Jewish Studies yet existed at an American university, or elsewhere, at the turn of the twentieth century. Stern likens Bialik and Ravnitsky's *The Book of Legends* to a site of ingathering, a textual Zion. So, too, *The Jewish Encyclopedia* and Ginzberg's *The Legends of the Jews* may be read as an extra-mural open university, a site where the sources of Jewish learning were made available for the purposes of Jewish Studies.

In striking out against the Science of Judaism, therefore, Scholem has strong precedents in a turn of the twentieth century Jewish-Studies-without-a-name. His allegory of the gravesite is a reading of a particular passage in "On Rabbinic Literature" concerning Zunz's assessment of the Haskalah, the Jewish Enlightenment movement that grew up in the generation between Mendelssohn and the Wissenschaft group. Zunz remarks that "as rabbinic literature was on the decline, European literature was on the rise, and Jews began to be drawn to it. What remains of the former in this last fifty years is nothing but a language borrowed as an accessible and familiar garment for clothing ideas which are to prepare the way for the utter disappearance of rabbinic literature."[74] This view of the Haskalah is short-sighted, and Zunz's report of the demise of rabbinic literature, to paraphrase Mark Twain, is premature. But Scholem does not take issue with these judgments. The crux, rather, is the place of living scholarship in relation to its predecessors. For Zunz, the Haskalah is not the cause but the consequence of the death of rabbinic literature. The use of Hebrew by the *maskilim*, that is, Haskalah scholars, is a residue of Jewish learning but not a revival. Zunz then adds, "Precisely because Jews in our times—limiting ourselves to the Jews of Germany—are seizing upon German language and German learning [Bildung] with such earnestness and are thus, perhaps unwittingly, carrying the neo-Hebraic literature [i.e., rabbinic literature] *to its grave*, science steps in demanding an account of what has already been sealed away."[75] The atmosphere may be lugubrious, but Zunz reports that he is witnessing the burial of the dead, not of the living. German-language Wissenschaft may in fact be among the pallbearers, but as science its task is grave registry for a Jewish learning that "has *already* been sealed away."

In contrast to what he sees as the dispassionate stance of Jewish science, Scholem refers to the passion and indeed the anger of Zunz and Steinscheider. But if, as Scholem says, "they know how to love and to hate," it is not apparent from Zunz's picture of the funeral of rabbinic literature, nor does Scholem offer other concrete instances of the minor demonic note in their major texts. Instead, he appropriates and transforms the graveyard image: "Their books, the classical works of the Science of Judaism, are a kind of procession around the dead, although at times it seems the authors themselves are the ghosts of Old Israel, seeking their salvation while dancing among the graves."[76] The language of flowers will not suffice to speak for rage, nor is a voluntary attachment to the beloved dead sufficient to account for the claim that the dead—the violent dead, the unmourned—may make upon the living. But then the context has changed since Hess's time. The Damascus Affair is not the extermination of European Jewry.

Scholem's picture of demonic scholars in a danse macabre at a tomb in their midst, overtaken by the ghosts from that very crypt, is very nearly the expressionist vision of director Michael Waszynski, in Poland, in 1937, bringing *The Dybbuk* to the movie screen, the play by S. Ansky based on the latter's ethnographic work among the Jews of the early twentieth-century Russian Pale.[77] Scholem's idiom, however, is that of the Kabbalah, the long, intricate, and ongoing tradition of Jewish mysticism. Hence, he closes the passage with a direct allusion to the sixteenth-century kabbalist Isaac Luria's concept of the breaking of the vessels and scattering of the supernal sparks held therein: "These are the sparks of very great souls from the unredeemed shell of brilliance, from a world in which life and death are jumbled together."[78] Research into the Kabbalah, thus, is Scholem's proposal for resolving the third and most troubling contradiction in the Wissenschaft movement. But that is also to say that as a scholar of Kabbalah (not as a practicing kabbalist) who moved Jewish mysticism to the center of Jewish Studies, Scholem could claim a place for himself as a demon in the dance.

It would be possible to contest Scholem's genealogy. The allusion to Luria may be read as a transumption, in the language of literary theorist Harold Bloom, a reference that fetches a notable precursor from afar as a spokesperson for one's own position, while masking a more proximate influence whose acknowledgment would have put one's originality in doubt. The valorization of Dionysian revelry by Nietzsche, whose work Scholem absorbed in his youth, would be a candidate for the excluded middle term here. An admirer of both Nietzsche and Scholem, Bloom also referred to transumptive allusion as "the return of the dead" in a theoretical system that he also translated into Lurianic terms.[79]

The aim of Scholem's passage was to demonize Wissenschaft, reading against the predominant tone of its impassive rationality. He would rediscover in its less visible, unscientific moments a forerunner to his own work. Not unlike Arendt's meeting with Rahel, Scholem is engaged in a "Jewish search for a usable past."[80] The positing of Jewish antecedents—forebears whose Jewishness appears unimpeachable—allow Jews in the present to represent themselves as returning to rather than departing from the Jewish past.

The complexities of the return—more transformation than repetition—are condensed in David Biale's characterization of Scholem as a "counterhistorian." Biale observes that "modern historiography"—but more particularly Scholem's counterhistory—"is a new development in the history of commentary in which Kabbalah was an earlier stage."[81] From this he draws the more daring conclusion: "Scholem's transformation of the traditional Jewish notion of commentary into historiography suggests that he views historical science, no matter how 'secular' or rational, as the modern form of Judaism."[82] Practiced as counterhistory, Jewish Studies is a metaphorization of Jewish learning. Or, to put this otherwise, "counter-" does similar work for Jewish Studies to "post-" in other allied fields.

Scholem's sharp critique of Wissenschaft is both furthered and yet challenged in turn—the double logic of the "counter-"—when Susannah Heschel argues that counterhistory is itself the demonic strain of the Science of Judaism. Heschel fights on two fronts in her study of Rabbi Abraham Geiger, the intellectual leader of the Reform movement and a

Wissenschaft historian. Heschel argues against Christian Hebraists who disputed the value of Hebrew Scriptures in the nineteenth century, and against Jewish neo-orthodoxies then and since that disparage the Reform movement as capitulation to Christian hegemony, by undermining the integrity of Hebrew Scriptures through their scientific, historical methods. For Heschel, the Christian historical argument by which the later supersedes the earlier is a counterhistory in itself. She contends that Geiger "sought to defend Judaism by writing a counterhistory of Christian counterhistory."[83] Simultaneously, Heschel defends Geiger, by writing a counterhistory of the Reform movement, vis-à-vis the detractors who depict Reform as a code word for assimilation.

Heschel concentrates attention on Geiger's contribution to the discussion among nineteenth-century Protestant scholars that shifted theological attention from "a supernatural Christ to a historical Jesus."[84] The foundation of Geiger's countermove is conveyed, however, in a statement in which he asserts that "the idea must come to the fore in full individual definiteness and in accordance with the language and concepts of the people with whom it originated; indeed, it must come forth as the particular expression of that people."[85] Geiger demonstrates that the teachings of the historical Jesus were wholly derivative of the milieu of Pharasaic Judaism. Historical science would put Christian theology between a rock and a hard place. Looking back, the great original was and remained Judaism. Geiger draws closer to his Christian adversaries when he admits that an original idea can become "independent of the soil in which it first matured," in which case the inaugural embodiment of the idea will be "transfigured into a greater spirituality."[86] Even so, on those grounds, the greatest spirituality would inhere where the soil of historical context was most transcended. Looking forward, that privileged position belonged not to hegemonic Christendom, but to the more thoroughly deracinated Reform Judaism. "Liberalizing Judaism," as Heschel characterizes it, "constituted not only a recovery of authentic Pharisaic religion but also a restoration of the faith of Jesus."[87]

Heschel adds that Geiger further challenged his Christian adversaries on methodological grounds. He pointed to the Christian theologians' "ignorance of a vast quantity of primary source materials—rabbinic literature—and hence of the limitations of their historical reconstructions. Their persistence thus became no longer a mark of involuntary ignorance, but a deliberate effort to present a false record as the truth."[88] In locating truth claims historically, Geiger was able to reverse the assault on the Talmud and other rabbinic writings that dated back to the Middle Ages. In this light, stiff-necked Christian historians appear to be stubbornly devoted to the testimony of later and lesser historical sources, whereas Jews had direct access to the older and more vital historical testament of Jewish learning.

Counterhistory, whether that of Geiger in the nineteenth century, that of Heschel in the current state of the question, or that of Scholem at a cusp between the two eras, remains history. Counterhistory undertakes a movement through and beyond certain theories and practices of history—especially Christian supersessionism, but also the antiquarianism and hyper-rationalism of the Science of Judaism—that occasions their rethinking or undoing from within.

In closing a counterhistorical account of the consensus view of the formation of Jewish Studies, it is important to recall that historiography, and not only its counter, continued to flourish through the period of its discontents, and remains a predominant discipline in the current state of the question.[89] Scholem himself, after all, places limits on the "counter-" to Jewish Science in his own historical project when he confessed in 1944 in his "Reflections on Modern Jewish Studies": "We came as rebels and we found ourselves to be heirs."[90] But some came as heirs, and were found to be rebels, chief among them Galician-born Salo W. Baron, who occupied the newly endowed Miller Chair in Jewish Studies at Columbia University in New York in 1928, which—along with the creation of the Littauer Chair at Harvard three years earlier, occupied by scholar of Jewish philosophy Harry Wolfson, born in Belorussia—marked an institutional inauguration for the field of Jewish Studies in the United States. Baron used his visibility and prestige to help establish the American Academy for Jewish Research, a national organization designed to build bridges between scholars teaching in diverse Jewish institutions, including rabbinical seminaries and Hebrew teachers colleges, and thus to begin to develop a network of scholars studying Jews. Baron also played a crucial role in broadening Jewish Studies beyond its initial disciplinary foundation in historiography. He joined with a group of Jewish social scientists, who were not studying Jews in their academic research, to found the Conference on Jewish Social Studies. Designed to provide data in part as an antidote to antisemitic attacks, the conference's journal, *Jewish Social Studies*, soon established itself as a leading venue for social scientific study of Jews.

While Baron's comprehensive, multivolume *A Social and Religious History of the Jews*[91] can be seen to take its place along the path opened by the Wissenschaft movement, his fundamental understanding of Jewish history stands in stark contrast to Jost's "inner unity" and Graetz's "single idea." Contemporary historian Michael Meyer rejected Baron's historical scheme, which, in Meyer's view, "destroys the possibility of a unified treatment."[92] Meyer goes on to explain: "While Baron's work enhances our knowledge of the particular themes he has chosen, his methodology is not conducive to revealing the dynamics of Jewish history and the connections among the diverse elements. Having contributed much to preparing the way for a profound, new, synthetic view of Jewish history, his conception and its execution have not been able to provide that synthesis."[93]

But where Meyer finds Baron wanting, judged against the background of Wissenschaft historicism, Baron may be seen to be writing Jewish history in what was then, and perhaps remains, a new key. Countering the drive toward a unifying concept, Baron emphasizes the heterogeneity of local detail. The approach is substantially articulated at the historical boundary that circumscribes the early period in which the terms of debate in Jewish Studies were first forged. In 1942, explicitly contesting the Nazis' racial definition of Jews, Baron offers a new key word for studying Jews: *community*. And in *The Jewish Community*, Baron provides the outline of a social history that focuses upon "an almost infinite variety of Jewish corporate bodies, assuming statutory forms and adopting modes of worship and ritual, according to their own decision, limited only by the power of custom," in antiquity no less than in modernity.[94] Baron remains committed to a vision of historical evolution departing from a single point of origin that leaves "its indelible imprint."[95] But inasmuch as the enduring trace is seen to be the organization of Jews as communities, each with its local stamp—rather than an overarching "Jewish people," much less a "Jewish race"—he gives grounds for plural and pluralistic *histories of Jews*, which are only now being written.

Baron opens the work by putting his own key words in question. "'Jewish community' has become an equivocal concept," he writes, and perhaps it is only when terms become equivocal that they become key. "It embodies the wide variety of meanings generally attached in sociological and juristic literature to the term community," he continues. "The complexity of connotations has moreover been increased by uncertainties associated with the adjective 'Jewish.'"[96] The uncertainties of the adjective continue to define the field, as "Jewish" remains the chief term of debate in Jewish Studies.

## Others Studying, Other Jews

In an influential work in contemporary Jewish Studies, historian Todd M. Endelman challenged Zunz's research agenda centering on "rabbinic literature."[97] The terms "rabbinic" and "literature," both separately and together, limit debate to the elite culture of texts. Endelman was more interested in boxing Jews than learning Jews. Students of European culture may find it surprising that social history, though by no means unprecedented in Jewish Studies,[98] was still struggling against the Science of Judaism model at such a late date. Students of Jewish Studies are perhaps not surprised enough that it also required special pleading to make room for the England of Isaac Watts's steam engine onto the map of modernity in the field. When Endelman declares that "there was no single path from tradition to modernity," he offers a rebuttal to a position in Jewish Studies no less ingrained than the emphasis on texts.[99] The single path had always departed from Berlin, running across Mendelssohn's chessboard and the historical research of the Science of Judaism.

Referring to Endelman at the close of a survey of Jewish culture in seventeenth-century Amsterdam, historian Yosef Kaplan speaks for "an alternative path to modernity."[100] Yet the very formulation, "an alternative," implies that *the* path remains the same. Thus, in framing his counterhistory as a revision of Jacob Katz's foundational social history, Kaplan ratifies the logic of center and periphery examined critically by Dipesh Chakrabarty in his contribution to postcolonial theory. Chakrabarty attempts to locate Indian history and historiography in relation to the hegemonic center he calls "Europe." For Chakrabarty, "Europe" is "both indispensable and inadequate" to the practice of historical inquiry of the peripheries.[101] It is inadequate because many Indian life practices originate and develop independently of European history. One will not achieve an understanding of the social gathering of the Bengali *adah* by fitting this conversational practice onto the grid of the French salon, British coffeehouse, or the Jewish open houses in Berlin.

In admitting "indispensability," however, Chakrabarty limits Indian Studies to participating in a debate whose terms were defined in "Europe." As an Indian historian, Chakrabarty may well choose to study the conversational practice of the *adah*, but the result will be considered "history," he says, only as judged according to those norms that first emerged in nineteenth-century German universities—the same norms internalized by the Science of Judaism. "Europe," in the sense of Christendom, has remained just as indispensable to Jewish Studies as to Indian Studies, in history and virtually all the constituent disciplines. But on the map of Jewish Studies, "Europe" has meant primarily Ashkenaz, Central and Eastern European Jewish communities, roughly coextensive in geography with the native lands and subsequent displacement and extension of Yiddish as a vernacular. Studying Ashkenazi Jews has had much the same hegemonic force within Jewish Studies as studying Europe has had in other fields.

Given the constraints of historical debate, Chakrabarty proposes that the only effective, if limited, countermove is to historicize "Europe" itself, that is, to demonstrate that modes of thought that "Europe" purveys as universal, such as rationality, are in fact local phenomena. Chakrabarty calls that project "provincializing Europe." Jewish Studies in a new key would provincialize Ashkenaz. To retrieve the terms of debate discussed in the preceding section, a counterhistory of the formative period in Jewish Studies is called for, no longer accepting the consensual but still arbitrary limitation to German-speaking lands. The following account is not a comprehensive integration of German Jewish scholarship and its others, but rather returns to the nineteenth century to map a different locus for an incipient Jewish Studies: a different cultural context and, therefore, different concerns. This account, then, is not an extension of the previous sections along a progressive chronological line. It is "post-Ashkenazic"—to deploy a prefix that moves beyond the dialectical thrust of the "counter"—seeking to bring to the fore alternative approaches and understandings that are erased when studying Ashkenaz is universalized as if it were coextensive with studying Jews.

Counter- or post-, the stakes involved in provincializing Ashkenaz are clearly enunciated by poet, translator, and essayist Ammiel Alcalay.[102] As his title suggests, Alcalay's "Exploding Identities" is a demonic text in the sense defined by Scholem: a construction that proceeds as a furious destruction. He offers a survey of Jewish Studies from the perspective of Sephardic and other cultural traditions beyond Ashkenaz. "The perpetuation of one narrative (or at least one set of constituent terms through which versions of that narrative are told), replete with experts armed with all the 'required' data, only serves to police the borders of a policy of separate development," writes Alcalay. "This move away from the multiply constructed contexts of textuality and more toward entrenchment into narrowly defined territories, small fiefdoms of power composed of self-serving and 'self-evident' truths, obscures the ways we have come to accept the 'infallibility' of those very 'truths,'" he continues. The narrowing of perspective, he concludes, "preempts even the possibility of raising precisely the kinds of issues that not only need to be raised but that the very materials under scrutiny *demand* to be raised."[103] It is customary to tell the story of Jewish Studies as a history of exclusion from "fiefdoms of power," but even where this view is persuasive, it does not obviate consideration of the differential positions of power *within* the field.

Alcalay illustrates the point by reference to the Ashkenazi-centric presuppositions to be found in figures of the first order in Jewish Studies. To cite the most esteemed case, Alcalay reproduces the following passage from literary critic and biblical translator Robert Alter's *Hebrew and Modernity*: "That is to say, by the late eighteenth century, European Jewry was launching the radical historical transformation we call modernization, and what was at issue now in the act of writing Hebrew was not just an aesthetic pursuit but a programmatic renegotiation of the terms of Jewish collective identity."[104] Having recognized that Alter is "resolutely sensitive to the nuances and resonances of Hebrew literature in its Eastern and Western European contexts," and acknowledging, moreover, "his informed readings in the diversity of premodern Mediterranean and Levantine Hebrew writing," Alcalay nevertheless discerns an implicit, fundamental, and unquestioned claim, even in Alter's work, that posits Ashkenazic Jews as the "truer" embodiment of "'modernity' proper."[105]

Deconstructive skepticism might well redouble the cautionary quotation marks, questioning the propriety of the "proper" in Alter's formulation. But even the conservative historical scholarship of Ismar Schorsch, long director of the Jewish Theological Seminary in New York, gives cogent evidence for a permeable border around Ashkenazic scholarship. Schorsch posits a "Sephardic curriculum," whose emphasis on grammar as a tool for scriptural interpretation, based ultimately on Jewish contact with Arabic literary studies in medieval Iberia, was crucial to the modernizing transformation of Jewish learning in Mendelssohn's Berlin.[106] Schorsch argues that Ashkenazic scholars turned to the Sephardic curriculum to find leverage in their efforts to break free of the provincial, Ashkenazic understanding of Jewish learning. Nor was this interest restricted to scholarship. The poet Heinrich Heine, who participated in the original Wissenschaft circle, also drew upon a Sephardic curriculum, fleetingly in his prose narrative "The Rabbi of Bachrach" of 1840, the year of the Damascus Affair, and with sustained engagement in his poem "Jehuda Halevy" from the "Hebrew Melodies" section of his late collection *Romanzero* (1851).

Moreover, like the surrounding hegemonic European cultures, Ashkenazic Jewish culture, especially in German-speaking lands, came to define the "proper" of "modernity" in large measure in a contrasting, self-valorizing relationship to an exotic Eastern, "premodern" Other.[107] "Jewish Orientalism" had its own particularities, however, in that the line of demarcation between the "modern West" and the "premodern East" ran through Jewish communities. Central European Ashkenazim represented themselves in contradistinction to their "oriental" Jewish contemporaries from Eastern Europe, as historian Steven E. Aschheim details; while "French Jews colonize Algerian Jews," in the argument of historian Elizabeth Friedman.[108] That is, French Jews compiled a report studying Algerian Jews for the French War Ministry as early as 1841, recommending the extension of French law and also the metropolitan system of Jewish consistories to colonial Algeria. The Algerian Jews resisted, notes Friedman; among other things, "the communities in Oran and

Constantine refused to bury French Jews in their cemeteries"[109]—a countermove even more demonic than Scholem imagined. And yet despite
deprecatory attitudes toward contemporary "orientals," Central
European Ashkenazi modernity found a usable past in their "Eastern"
ancestry—as opposed to the "Western" heritage of Greece and Rome—
especially evident in nineteenth-century Reform synagogue architecture.
Following the course of that architectural history, art historian Olga Bush
has traced the complexities of Ashkenazi orientalism as it crossed from
Europe to the United States where the East–West divide was further com-
plicated by distinctions between settled and immigrant Jews, uptown and
downtown Jews, and the new context of American culture.[110] In sum, it is
possible to provincialize Ashkenaz by studying its constant interaction
with other Jews beyond its borders.

Alcalay advocates a further theoretical approach by reference to
debates in Croatian and Serbian letters: "a different historical formation,
polycentric and polymorphous."[111] All the heterogeneous Jewish communities are thus viewed as provincial centers, and Ashkenaz becomes but
one of the provinces. Ensuing comparisons would no longer presuppose
the normativity of Ashkenazic history. This epistemological project is
openly political. "To be 'abbreviated' in the multiplicity of our possible
range of identities is a form of oppression," writes Alcalay.[112] Like Koltun-
Fromm in his discussion of Hess, Alcalay has recourse to the key word
"identity"; it is the language of the current state of the question. The project of provincializing Ashkenaz is a form of practicing Jewish Studies as
liberation politics, though the liberation is now from within.

A polycentric approach would recast the formation of Jewish Studies,
even where history is retained as the disciplinary framework. One might
follow, for example, the course of the travels of Rabbi David d'Beth Hillel
from Jerusalem to Madras, published in 1832, as he studies Jews in the
communities he finds along the way;[113] or the Inquisitorial records of the
trials of crypto-Jews attempting and ultimately failing to elude prosecu-
tion over the breadth of colonial Spanish America.[114]

Spain also offers a test case for a polycentric revision. Aside from rabid
denunciations of Jews and Judaism, studying Jews in Spain had to await
the formal abolition of the Spanish Inquisition in 1834. After all, sympathetic treatment would have risked suspicion of judaizing, which the
Inquisition was empowered to discover and eliminate. Hardly a decade
passed, however, when José Amador de los Ríos began to publish a series
of journal articles in November 1845, which would eventually result in
his *Historical, Political, and Literary Studies of the Jews of Spain* in 1848.
In nineteenth-century France, the inaugural work in modern Jewish
Studies can be traced through German-trained Jewish scholars of Semitic

languages, Solomon Munk and Joseph Naftali Derenbourg, directly back along the path that departs from the German milieu of the Science of Judaism. Not so Amador de los Ríos: he comes to studying Jews from his interest in the architectural monuments of Spain. Perhaps more to the point, the Inquisition may have ended, but the Edict of Expulsion of 1492 was still in force, so there were, in principle, no Jews to study in nineteenth-century Spain. Spanish Jewish Studies begins with others, that is, non-Jews, studying Jews in an intellectual and institutional environment quite different from the beginnings of the Science of Judaism in Germany.

The distinctive characteristic of this province of Jewish Studies is already enunciated by Amador de los Ríos as the leading question that his voluminous study intends to answer. Can Spanish history be properly understood without studying Iberian Jews? To this epistemological issue, he adds an ethical concern: "Is there justice in such disdain and neglect . . . ?"[115] The former question might be addressed by intellectual perspicacity, but the latter calls for "impartiality," as he stresses both in 1848, and in the greatly augmented, indeed quite new work of 1878, under a revised title that gives pride of place to history: *Social, Political, and Religious History of the Jews of Spain and Portugal.* Studying Jews had been obstructed because "all feeling of impartiality and justice [was] drowned in the black vortex of the most impassioned and intolerant fanaticism," he noted in 1878.[116]

Amador de los Ríos invokes the stance of impartiality to serve a juridical function: to "call to judgment the past centuries in order to demand an accounting and a reason for their ideas and their deeds, pronouncing at last a rightful and inescapable sentence."[117] There are no Jews for Spanish Jewish Studies to liberate. But the juridical function may be seen to exercise a retroactive force in a historical court of appeals that might overturn the prior verdict of the Inquisition.

It is nothing less than startling, therefore, to find at the very close of the first edition of Amador de los Ríos's defense the following declaration: "The dispersion of the Hebrew people is not an event which, like the enslavement of Poland, depends upon the will of men. It is the consummation of the prophecies, the fulfillment of the word of God; and it is in vain that the God-killing people will struggle to withdraw itself from that immutable decree."[118] As Immanuel Wolf wrote in "On the Concept of the Science of Judaism" (1822) in the original publishing organ of the Science of Judaism movement, "Christian scholars, however great their merit in the development of individual aspects of Judaism, have almost always treated Judaism for the sake of a historical understanding of Christian theology."[119] Reading the concluding charge of "Christ-killers" from a scholar studying Jews under the banner of impartiality gives pause.

If not proposing something like a categorical imperative against instrumentalizing Jews in the service of other fields of study, one might at least note the importance of Jewish Studies as an open house for scholarship in which Jews are the hosts and not the guests. On the other hand, it is noteworthy that Amador de los Ríos expunged the concluding Christian theology and the attendant charge against Jews when he rewrote his revised edition. It would appear that his years of studying Jews served to overcome his initial prejudices—anecdotal evidence in favor of keeping the house of Jewish Studies open.

The later and by far more widely recognized contribution to studying Jews in Spain by literary scholar and cultural historian Américo Castro forms part of the varied drive to revise historiography in the period of Arendt, Scholem, and Benjamin. Castro's thesis, elaborated most thoroughly in *The Structure of Spanish History*,[120] is often adulterated as a picture of peaceful, even cheerful coexistence between Christians, Muslims, and Jews in medieval Iberia—very good for travel brochures. Rather than constructing an idyllic past, however, Castro himself seeks a theoretical model for "the Christian-Islamic-Judaic contexture, within which it was no longer possible to recognize anything that is pure and abstract Christianity, Islamism, or Judaism."[121]

One catches the polemical edge of the word "pure." Having terrorized Jewish communities in the pogroms that raged across the Iberian Peninsula in 1391, the Christian regimes faced the mixed blessing of massive conversion for a full century before the expulsion. One result was a coexistence—sometimes amicable, sometimes hostile—between those who remained Jews and those who converted. Indeed, the dividing line ran between individual family members who often remained in close contact. The Spanish Inquisition aimed at defending that border, to prevent "backsliding" by converts and their descendents, still deemed "New Christians" even after many generations, and to punish judaizers, those who reverted to Jewish ways. From this effort arose the ideology and statutes of "blood purity," which transformed religious policing into racial profiling. And as we know, profiling leads back to policing. Those with "Jewish blood" were suspect of judaizing.

So Castro deliberately overtakes and upends the language of purity that is the foundation of what Amador de los Ríos already saw as the neglect of and disdain for studying Jews. In reaction, then, to racializing ideologies of purity and the penchant in science for isolating operant factors, Castro works out a theory of cultural heterogeneity in an environmentalist paradigm whose key word is "morada," dwelling place.

Castro's leading question remains, "What is the meaning of the term 'Spanish' . . . ?"[122] His answer is that "Spanish" refers not to a putative biological category, but rather to an environment characterized by the close contact of Christians, Muslims, and Jews. They dwelled together for nearly eight centuries, primarily in conflict, but always exercising reciprocal influences. Both the question and the answer, whether in Castro or in Amador de los Ríos, open intellectual space for studying Jews that emerges from a distinctive relationship between modern scholarship and, here, Catholic theology. And while Castro's approach met with very significant resistance by proponents of a "pure and abstract" Visigothic base for Spanish history (i.e., purely and by no means abstractly Christian), it has carried the day. By now, decades of scholarship on the formation of Spain devote attention to studying Jews as an integrated component.[123]

Castro's historical practice with respect to Jews, it needs be noted, falls short of his theory. The concept of the mixed dwelling place should have guided his research into the Jewish elements of "Spanish-ness" no less than the Christian. One would not expect a claim to distinguish a "pure and abstract" Jewish ingredient that was later added to the Spanish mix. But one would have expected Castro to historicize Jewish practices in the environments in which Jews were most at home, rather than to make inferences about Jewish communities from Christian practices on the premise that all things Spanish must have some Jewish element. Concretely, Castro imputes the origins of the Spanish Inquisition itself to "the totalitarian religiosity of the Moors, and, especially, the Jews."[124]

The egregious error has been soundly debunked by historian Benzion Netanyahu, who has demonstrated that Castro did not study Jewish legal proceedings in their own terms, which is to say in their own dwelling place.[125] The error appears only the more tendentious when one recalls that Castro had at his disposal the work of German-born Israeli historian Yitzhak Baer, who published relevant primary sources along with the original German edition of his *History of the Jews of Christian Spain* (1929), and analyzed them within the context of Jewish history.[126] Indeed, Castro quotes Baer. Again, even in the absence of theological apologetics, the question of who is the host of the dwelling place has its impact. It is Baer, not Castro, who has become the cornerstone for studying Iberian Jews in the context of Jewish Studies.

The shortcomings of Castro's particular analyses need not obscure the value of his theoretical paradigm, nor the potential impact on Jewish Studies of provincializing Ashkenaz. The legacy of the Science of Judaism tends toward studying Jews in isolation. Against that background, efforts to conceive of Jewish life as integrated in and contributing to a larger and primarily non-Jewish society have generally been viewed as antithetical in the Ashkenazi-centric paradigm.[127] Starting out from Sepharad, one finds a mode of studying Jews as integrated participants in a mixed national history.

The paradigm of hybridity in the Sephardic context calls for two further observations. First, Iberian Jews were not, of course, only "of Christian Spain," to recall Baer's title. Muslims controlled most of the Peninsula for at least three centuries and some of the area for several centuries more, and Jews lived among them. Indeed, what is usually thought of as the Golden Age of "Spanish" Jewry is Judeo-Arabic culture. Even when the first significant wave of Separdic Jewish exiles fled the Iberian Peninsula in the wake of a renewed Muslim invasion, the refugees generally resettled in more tolerant North African Muslim dominions and so maintained and reinforced their ties to Arabic-language cultures. Maimonides, the greatest Jewish scholar of the medieval period, is the exemplary case: born and educated in Muslim Cordoba, settling eventually in Cairo and writing much of his work in Arabic.

Reviewing scholarship on relations between Muslims and Jews, Mark R. Cohen underlines how evaluations of the past fluctuate according to the political mood of the present.[128] Nevertheless, Cohen speaks for a consensus when he declares that on the whole, Jews fared better under crescent than under cross throughout history. So, one might infer that it was the Muslim dwelling place of al-Andalus, rather than the Christian dwelling place of Castille, that created the historical preconditions for a theory of hybridity in Sephardic studies. Alcalay's denunciation of "abbreviated possibilities" occasioned by the hegemony of Ashkenaz, therefore, touches especially on the potential benefits to Jewish Studies of developing its cultural paradigms by studying the Judeo-Arabic heritage,[129] rather than to return ever and again to the dwelling place among Christians.

A second observation with respect to provincializing Ashkenaz is to note that in Sephardic studies heterogeneity is not limited to the relationship between Jews and others, but rather also includes other Jews. Even before the time of Amador de los Ríos, studying Jews in the Iberian context has included studying Jewish converts to Christianity and their descendants, referred to most often as *marranos* or *conversos*. The nature of clandestine Jewish religious observance on their part has long been a point of debate.[130] Photographer and director Frederic Brenner's contribution to that discussion, the documentary film *The Last Marranos*,[131] refocuses the historical discussion as a contemporary issue when he represents surviving crypto-Jewish practices in Belmonte, Portugal, at the moment when open and authorized Jewish worship was being reestablished in the country after five centuries. Brenner's work may also stand as an example of the efficacy and increasing importance of the medium of documentary film in the present state of Jewish Studies.

Beyond religious practice, historian Henry Kamen marks the wide scope given to the issue by reference to Baer's *History of the Jews in Christian Spain*: "Baer states uncompromisingly that 'the conversos and Jews were one people, united by destiny.'"[132]

Neither "destiny" nor Arendt's related term, "fate," has ever gained much traction in Jewish Studies—the legacy of Jewish *science* mitigates against them—but the concept of Jewish unity, often formulated in the expression "one people," has been and remains a key. The inclusion of marranos in that unity is a step toward a more diversified view, but it does not necessarily defend the particularities of the marrano experience from erasure. The one Hebrew word, *Adonay*, on the lips of an elderly woman in prayer in Brenner's documentary, despite five hundred years of suppression, demonstrates a remarkable and moving continuity; but the accompanying gestures, patterned on Catholic rites, are no less striking as manifestations of marrano difference. The underlying theological commitment to the oneness of God notwithstanding, marrano life practices and historical experience resist inclusion under the heading of commonality. The point of provincializing Ashkenaz, and then provincializing Sepharad in turn—remarking on "polycentric and polymorphous" experiences of Iberian Jews—is to reexamine all formulations of unity as a usually tendentious narrowing of real heterogeneity, and to rediscover the many Jewish peoples who consider themselves, in their various ways, one people.

# 2      State of the Question

## Jewish Studies after Auschwitz

A current state is a state "for now," a state of our own conceiving, but also a transient matter. The ancients taught the enduring quality of wisdom traditions, social practices, and structures of power. What the moderns learn from that lesson, however, is that even the most enduring of ancient constructions comes to an end: all things human are only for now. Modernity represents itself as the aftermath of those endings.

The chief discipline for charting and explaining the overarching pattern of ruptures in continuity (more or less acute, more or less complete), followed by innovation or transformation, is modern history. For well over a century, historiography and the related disciplines of philology and archaeology predominated in Jewish Studies as a modern field, a scientific project separate from covenantal obligations. Science was the key word in Jewish Studies in the nineteenth century, and history the key mode of studying Jews scientifically, not as an eternal people circumscribed by a providential design, but as a changing people, acting on their own behalf in an open-ended story within the constraints of different social environments.

The rupture that distinguishes the current state of Jewish Studies from its predecessors is the "war against the Jews, 1933–1945," in historian Lucy Dawidowicz's pointed phrase.[1] To call that twelve-year period by either of its most common names—the English designation Holocaust, based on a Greek root referring to a whole, burnt, sacrificial offering, or the Hebrew *Shoah*, literally "catastrophe"—is already to locate discussion in one of many positions within contemporary terms of debate. Key words are more than lexical niceties. They concentrate disparate meanings at a point of possible intersection; they make certain conversations possible, while obstructing others; they bear a heavy burden. For an English-language text, Shoah is perhaps the better term, at least in that it signals resistance to any easy comprehension.

To speak of genocide, another key word coined precisely on the basis of the Nazi attempt to exterminate Jews, is by no means neutral. "Genocide," too, has a history whose salient point is institutional. Polish Jewish lawyer Raphael Lemkin introduced the term in the *United Nations*

*Convention on the Prevention and Punishment of the Crime of Genocide* of 1948 that defined certain acts against peoples as a particular kind of international crime. The choice of Latin roots for the neologism as a means of speaking to and for an international body imports a history of Roman Empire and Church of Rome, that is, a foundational perspective in which "Europe" is seen as universal. The term is no less debatable than the others. But the institutional purposes of creating a definition that would make it possible to recognize similarities between the Shoah and future atrocities also implies that the Jewish genocide of the Nazi years is only a rupture "for now," that it forms part of a series of similar events: prior, yet to come, or ongoing in the current state.

Theological alternatives to historical study have been articulated from the very time of the events, before such terms as Holocaust and Shoah came to take a place in current debate. In *Night*, for instance, a text that raised novelist and essayist Elie Wiesel to prominence as a spokesperson for victims of the Shoah, the death by hanging of a Jewish boy at Auschwitz transcends the juridical context that underwrites the concept of genocide. Unlike most of the manifold ways in which countless murders were committed, that hanging is staged as the execution of a judicial sentence: the false, summary military justice of the Nazis. The issue for the camp inmates, as Wiesel retells it, is the apparent withdrawal of God—a negative counterpart to the divine interventions of miracles. "Where is God now?" a Jewish prisoner asks: "And I heard a voice within me answer him: 'Where is He? Here He is—He is hanging here on this gallows.'"[2] Neither miracles nor the death of God are historical constructions.

Literary critic, philosopher, and cultural historian Walter Benjamin, writing in the face of a triumphant fascism in 1940, and soon to be its victim, sounds a call for scholarly engagement. In a critique of nineteenth-century German historicism, which could well be extended to the major scholarship of the Science of Judaism, Benjamin asserts: "The only historian capable of fanning the spark of hope in the past is the one who is firmly convinced that *even the dead* will not be safe from the enemy if he is victorious. And this enemy has not ceased to be victorious."[3] Benjamin conceives of the recovery of the spark of hope otherwise buried with the victims of history as a *"weak* messianic power"[4]—a strong form would perhaps be to fan the sparks hidden in the present. In the current state of Jewish Studies, historian Yehuda Bauer does not deploy Benjamin's theo-political idiom, but he nonetheless takes up the "weak messianic" task when he argues against those who see the Shoah as an ineffable and unfathomably unique phenomenon.[5] Such a more openly religious stance removes the atrocities from human history, he maintains, and so represents a past from which humanity cannot learn—extinguishing the sparks of hope. Historicizing the Shoah, Bauer contends, is the means of defending the future against its recurrence, whether as a renewed war against the Jews or any other genocidal violence.

Historian Deborah Lipstadt has raised a cautionary note concerning the move from classroom to wholly unmetaphorical courtroom, particularly with regard to Holocaust denial. She avers that "when the court is asked to render a decision not on a point of law . . . but on a point of history," the situation "transforms the legal arena into a historical forum, something the courtroom was never designed to be." Lipstadt then adds, "When historical disputes become lawsuits, the outcome is unpredictable,"[6] though fortunately, when she herself went to trial in the well-publicized case contesting Holocaust denial in 1996, the court found in her favor. Yet unpredictable judgments notwithstanding, the courtroom has always been the scene of historical reconstruction, usually of the recent past. The Nuremburg trials of Nazi war criminals from 1945 to 1949 were an early effort of historical investigation, and the published proceedings, like the records of the Inquisition, are a sourcebook for continuing research. Thus trials make history in more than one sense. But the converse also holds. Historiography in Jewish Studies often finds an implicit paradigm in legal proceedings, particularly with respect to the history of anti-Jewish and antisemitic assaults. It is well to recall that Amador de los Ríos already conceived of his inaugural contribution to studying Jews in nineteenth-century Spain as a posthumous defense against the ceaseless triumph of the Inquisition in banning Jews from Spanish history.

The judicial subtext is patent in the first major publication in what has come to be called Holocaust studies in the United States, historian Raul Hilberg's *The Destruction of the European Jews* (1961).[7] Hilberg discloses the modus operandi of the crime and, wherever possible, the names of the criminals. To this end, the admissible evidence is constituted by documents from the vast archives of Nazi bureaucracy. This is not to say that Hilberg accepted Nazi military orders and civilian directives at face value. On the contrary, he made a signal contribution by deciphering the coded language of their systematic deceptions. Nevertheless, Hilberg reserves agency and voice—the capacity to initiate action on the basis of one's own will and the authority to depict that action from one's own perspective—all but exclusively to the Nazis and their accomplices.

Hilberg's restricted view of agency made Nazi violence the subject of his history, which, once again, left little room for Jews. As subjects endowed with agency, they appear primarily as collaborators in their own demise—an explicit thesis in his work. Hilberg's collaborationist thesis depended upon his finding that there was little violent self-defense by Jews, which is to say Jews did not take up the only active role that his terms envisioned. The accusation of a criminal passivity raised against Jewish victims had support from other quarters: Arendt's *Eichmann in Jerusalem,* for instance, and more generally the Zionist condemnation of European Jews "going like sheep to the slaughter."

Bauer has challenged that baleful thesis by studying Jewish resistance.[8] On the one hand, he demonstrated that Hilberg had overlooked the widespread participation of Jews in armed revolt against the Nazis, not only in the most famous case in the Warsaw Ghetto Uprising but throughout Europe. More important, Bauer expanded the scope of the term, so that resistance can be seen to include many activities beyond the notion of armed struggle. These salutary corrections expand Hilberg's thesis, but without countering the orientation around resistance. The contributions of popular culture have been largely circumscribed by those terms, and at the most popular, the search for a plausible subject of successful resistance led director Steven Spielberg along the same lines as Hilberg, though in the opposite direction. The Nazis alone had agency for Hilberg, which they used for the purposes of destruction; but, in principle, that agency could have been directed toward the good. The bad Nazi spoke out against the Jews; the good Nazi speaks for them, appropriates the voice of the Jews. Spielberg's Schindler not only says "we" when referring to the situation of the Jews in his employ in his climactic oration, he is even allowed to give a lesson on Sabbath observance to a rabbi.[9]

Essayist, memoirist, novelist, and Jewish camp survivor Primo Levi, and philosopher and cultural theorist Giorgio Agamben in his wake, countered the emphasis on resistance in the study of the Shoah by focusing attention on the *Muselmänner* (literally "Muslims," though the etymology has yet to be fully elucidated), the term used by camp inmates to designate those who were so extenuated by exhaustion and starvation that they were beyond resistance of even the most minimal kind.[10] If Muselmänner cannot be defended by Jewish Studies, the enemy will not have ceased to be victorious, and philosopher Emil Fackenheim's "614th commandment" will remain unfulfilled: "The authentic Jew of today is forbidden to hand Hitler yet another, posthumous victory."[11]

To rethink Holocaust studies from the position of the Muselmänner, rather than the Warsaw Ghetto Uprising or Schindler's factory, is another case of reading the major through the minor. It is a limit case: the story of the extinguishing of agency and voice, which is to say a story that devolves into story-lessness.

In Claude Lanzmann's documentary film *Shoah,* the moment of silencing is a trauma that survivor Simon Srebnik is compelled to repeat.[12]

Lanzmann had brought Srebnik back to the site of the camp to film his testimony. The scene then shifts to a plaza outside a church in the nearby town. As the worshippers exit the church they are introduced to Srebnik, recognizing in him the boy who used to sing at the orders of the Nazis. The churchgoers greet him, expressing happiness that he has survived, that he has returned. But their recollections culminate in a diatribe: the Jews killed Christ; their murder by the Nazis was only what they deserved. Having first filmed Srebnik telling his story, Lanzmann now films his effacement amid the churchgoers, his silence, his enigmatic smile. For Levi and Agamben the key to the more extreme situation of the Muselmann is not resistance, but shame. In the shame of the Muselmann, of Srebnik, of Lanzmann, it is possible to hear a voice that is not a voice, to recuperate a humanity below the threshold of resistance, and so to fan the faintest sparks of hope.

Sociologist Eric R. Wolf articulated an influential theoretical model for addressing the narratological problem, when he proposed the means for studying what he called "peoples without history."[13] Wolf's argument had an overtly political edge. Subjugated peoples are defeated twice: first when they are conquered, and then in the continuing victory accomplished when the conquerors discount their ways of representing themselves. The subjugated peoples without a history legible to their conquerors are cast into the conceptual realm of the primitive, the backward, the premodern. To ally with subjugated peoples in the present—to recapture a place for them in the present—it is necessary to recognize forms of agency different from the hegemonic forms, and to hear a voice that represents itself otherwise than historically.

Wolf was not studying Jews. The Science of Judaism had long since learned to construct Jews historically and so to claim a place in the modernity of the powers ruling over Jews. But in the context of Holocaust studies, reading Hilberg and Spielberg and more generally the trials of the perpetrators through the limit case of the Muselmänner, one sees the risk that the Jewish victims of the Shoah may be victimized a second time as a people without history. The countermove has been to construct Jews as peoples with memory and so to reclaim a voice, where agency was missing.

The conceptual shift may be measured in relation to Hilberg's *The Destruction of the European Jews*. Hilberg himself played an editorial role in the English-language edition of *The Warsaw Diary of Adam Czerniakow*.[14] As the head of the Warsaw Jewish Council, Czerniakow would be judged a collaborator in light of Hilberg's earlier assessment. In his own voice, however, Czerniakow appears as a man deceived by the semblance of an active role staged for him by the Nazis. He committed suicide at the time of the massive deportations from Warsaw in 1942, when he found his power to act in defense of himself, his family, and his community had been a sham from the outset: a Muselmann with a title. The edition of Czerniakow's diary is representative of a large-scale effort to give voice to the victims, carried out at a seam between academic research and a general readership in Jewish Studies: the printing of myriad memoirs, sometimes at commercial publishing houses, sometimes at university presses, often with scholarly introductions. That effort has been augmented by videotape archives of survivor testimony, such as the collection organized by Spielberg.[15] A further contrast may speak for the whole. Hilberg eventually compiled a selection of archival materials upon which *The Destruction of the European Jews* had been built; his *Documents of Destruction* includes hardly a line written by a Jew.[16] Within five years, Dawidowicz edited *A Holocaust Reader*, an anthology of texts featuring the voices of Jewish victims; she writes in the preface to that volume, "The specter of the Holocaust continues to haunt Jews everywhere and to define their priorities." She adds, "The imperative is Jewish survival, above all, the security of Israel."[17]

The specter of annihilation and the counter-imperative of survival characterize contemporary Jewish Studies, well beyond the subfields of Holocaust studies and Israel studies. The haunting is so pervasive that it is pertinent to name the current period in Jewish Studies "after Auschwitz." The site of the greatest number of systematic killings, the death camp Auschwitz has become the part of the Shoah that most commonly stands for the whole; and used in that sense, the expression "after Auschwitz" has prompted sustained debate since it was employed in a polemical remark by philosopher Theodor W. Adorno in 1949: "To write poetry after Auschwitz is barbaric. And this corrodes even the knowledge of why it has become impossible to write poetry today."[18] Adorno subsequently revised his position when he reflected more than a decade later: "Perennial suffering has as much right to expression as a tortured man has to scream; hence it may have been wrong to say that after Auschwitz you could no longer write poems. But it is not wrong to raise the less cultural question whether after Auschwitz you can go on living."[19] Attentive to the ghosts of the Shoah, Jewish Studies in the current state of the question is a leading field in the politicized pedagogy that Adorno called "Education after Auschwitz."[20] For Adorno himself, still very much haunted by the specter of Jewish survival, the pedagogical goal after Auschwitz is a political defense against future fascisms.

More broadly, Jewish Studies entered its current stage, "characterized by rapid enrollment increases, subject expansion, and the emergence of separate Judaica departments," according to sociologists Paul Ritterband

and Harold S. Wechsler in the late 1960s.[21] The sudden albeit brief rise of Israel in world opinion as the underdog victors of the Six Day War in 1967 was a factor in that growth—recalling Dawidowicz's link between a general imperative of Jewish survival and the security of the State of Israel. But the shift that Ritterband and Wechsler chart from "the desire for social and religious recognition" of the earlier stages of Jewish Studies to a "survivalist" agenda meant to defend against the perceived threats of assimilation[22] is more closely related in the United States to the context of the politicized curriculum that grew out of the liberation movements in the 1960s: Black Studies, Latino and other ethnic studies, Women's Studies, and Queer Studies. Like these other fields in relation to their own constituent groups, and sometimes in alliance with them, Jewish Studies speaks for the survival of Jews as Jews against a curriculum that has otherwise subordinated Jews and other differences to white, Christian, heterosexual males. Jewish Studies both constructs Jews as a people with a history and reconstructs Jewish memory.

The impact is most visible in the emergence of identity and memory as key words, to be taken up in the next section of this chapter. Before closing the present discussion, however, three further observations serve to delimit the haunting.

The first observation is a historical note. Clearly, the Shoah ruptured developing debate in Jewish Studies in the most material sense. Many of the Jews to be studied were annihilated, their books burned, the artifacts of their life practices scattered, their memories buried—the objects of research vanished. So, too, many scholars perished who were studying Jews, like historians Simon Dubnow and Emmanuel Ringelblum.[23]

The second observation is preemptive. The predominant mode of historical understanding is progressive or, to use the founding, Christian language, supersessionist: one era closes off another, never to return; the later is New! And Improved! The relationship between history and the memory disciplines in Jewish Studies does not conform—not least, because historiography has not been superseded, but rather continues to be practiced in the field. Moreover, history has been strongly inflected by memory in the current state of the question, thus often departing markedly from the Science of Judaism model. It has been noted that social history made a belated appearance in Jewish Studies, but Baron's important example has also been cited as a precursor to the interdisciplinary conversation of sociology and history. A binary distinction will not hold.

Nevertheless, the threat of the disappearance of Jews as Jews extends back as a point of continuity across the rupture. In one of its forms, the concern was criticized by Baron as the "lachrymose" approach to Jewish history, a bemoaning, scholarly or otherwise, of the various destructions suffered by Jews, rather than an account, as Baron preferred, of cultural achievements. But the specter could also be invoked as a spur to renewal. It is thus that "survival" already appears as a key word in a debate of 1919 between Jewish philosophers Franz Rosenzweig and Martin Buber. Rosenzweig counterposes a reconceptualization of Jewish Law to Buber's prior revision of Jewish teaching in a letter, arguing against Buber's implicit acceptance of the boundaries traced by nineteenth-century neo-Orthodoxy around the "permissible," which left so much of modern Jewish life as "extra-Jewish."[24] Rosenzweig offered a flexible but still more holistic understanding of Jewish Law that would make all of life, again, a Jewish concern. He acknowledged that, taken as a temporary measure, the separation had a certain utility and a tradition, "where the security of Jewish life was at stake." He continues, "Only in modern times," however, "*when Jewish survival was considered perpetually at stake*, was this treatment of the law given a permanent status."[25] Well before Auschwitz, then, Rosenzweig defines Jewish modernity in terms of the survival imperative.

## The Boundaries of Ethnic Identity

Trauma challenges survival, even for one who lives on after calamity, because certain forms of rupture can be so profound that they raise the question of whether, or in what sense, one is the same after as one was before. "Identity" (from a Latin root for "same") emerged as a key word in both academic and popular culture to address that question and has become a central concept in Jewish Studies, as witnessed by the titles of countless books and articles in every discipline and subfield.

Reflecting on his seminal text of 1968, *Identity: Youth and Crisis*, from the vantage point of its republication more than two decades later, German-born Jewish psychoanalyst Erik H. Erikson outlines the theoretical development within its original therapeutic setting. Erikson had been treating former soldiers at the Mount Zion Veteran's Rehabilitation Clinic following the Second World War, he recalls, which places his contribution in a position parallel to Freud's work on veterans of the First World War. The compulsion to repeat the scene of wounding attested to in traumatic dreams contradicted Freud's major thesis of *The Interpretation of Dreams* (1900), according to which dreams always expressed wish fulfillments. In working through the consequences for psychoanalytic theory in *Beyond the Pleasure Principle* (1920), Freud expanded his view beyond war veterans and postulated a death drive as an element of normal psychology, in effect universalizing trauma by tracing it back into the earliest stages of organic life.

Erikson's initial observation stands close to Freud. Erikson writes: "Most of our patients, so we concluded at the time, had neither been 'shellshocked' nor become malingerers, but had through the exigencies of war lost a sense of personal sameness and historical continuity. They were impaired in that central control over themselves for which, in the psychoanalytic scheme, only the 'inner agency' of the ego could be held responsible. Therefore, I spoke of a loss of 'ego identity.'"[26] But his research, too, veered away from the acute trauma of war veterans to the normal developmental pattern that he construed in its image. Adolescents separating themselves from the haven of childhood also undergo a temporary, disorienting loss of sameness and continuity, which they overcome when they establish the self-control of full adulthood. The threat of discontinuity—compulsively reenacted by trauma victims, resolved more or less decisively in most other cases—is the implicit background against which identity was defined.

The concept of identity links much work in Jewish Studies to the broader curriculum. In the interests of highlighting common ground and so facilitating conversation across academic divisions, one may turn to Caroline Walker Bynum, a cultural and literary historian of medieval Christian Europe, for a useful synopsis of current identity theories. Bynum outlines three conceptual clusters. There is, first, a specifying function: approaches that emphasize the distinguishing elements that make for a unique individual. Second, there are theories that seek the grounds of "group affiliation" in shared elements and mutual recognition;[27] such affiliation also includes a specifying dimension, distinguishing affiliates of one group from those of another. Third, there is an issue of "spatiotemporal continuity" that makes it possible to assert, in Bynum's words, "I am the same person I was a moment ago."[28] The last of the three, but also the first, concerns the individual as the undivided— precisely that modern self differentiated sharply from social collectivities (e.g., guilds, tribes), on the one hand, and yet whose sameness and continuity are threatened by historical change, understood as rupture. The individuated identity of these clusters is the virtual patient of Erikson's therapy.

Bynum's second cluster stands out as a middle term in more ways than one, since definitions of group affiliation offer an understanding of identity between the individual self and a generalized humanity. From the time of the influential work of anthropologist Frederik Barth, contemporaneous with Erikson's most important publications,[29] the middle cluster has been articulated principally in terms of ethnicity. As a matter of group affiliation, identity opens onto the political issue that Arendt had decried in her analysis of Rahel and her times, when Jews embraced emancipation as personal liberation rather than insisting on entering modernity as a corporate entity.

But the tensions between theories of individual versus group identity persist beyond emancipation, as historian S. Ilan Troen illustrates in the debates over the construction of "a secular 'Jewish' education" in the independent State of Israel.[30] Troen cites a statement in the Knesset in 1959 by Minister of Education Zalman Aranne in evidence of the decided Zionist inclination toward a Jewish identity based on group affiliation. The questions that Aranne raises speak for various forms of understanding the relation of individuals to the group: "How to educate youngsters here for *loyalty* to the Jewish people . . . ? How to implant in youngsters here *a feeling of being part* of Jewish history . . . ? How to inculcate *Jewish Consciousness* . . . ? How to educate Israeli youth who receive their education in a non-religious school to *appreciate* the cultural heritage of the Jewish people which for most of its time has been suffused with religion?"[31] According to this program, a Zionist education in the State would create or reinforce a group identity in each young Jew, defined as heirs of—and therefore continuous with—a certain history (being part), which is valorized (appreciate). As a result, the individual will be charged with and accept an obligation (loyalty) to meet the demands of the imperative of Jewish survival.

Aranne recognizes the difficulties "here," in the State, that arise from the disjunction between Zionist ideology constructing Jews as a modern nation, and the European Jewish past, which he characterizes as "suffused with religion." Troen goes on to register a rather different challenge, however. Under the influence of the national model presented by the United States as a "melting pot" of immigrants, and the correlated American pedagogical model, "the contemporary version of 'Jewish Consciousness,'" as articulated in a Ministry of Education report of 1994, adopts an individualistic program, "whose key concepts are pluralism and identity."[32] Troen explains, "As employed by contemporary educators, 'identity' and 'pluralism' suggest choice. It is the child and youth who decides what he or she is to become from a range of choices provided by the schools. This includes the Jewishness of his or her choice or even no Jewishness at all. This possibility stands in contrast, if not contradiction, to the way 'Jewish Consciousness' as a collective phenomenon was originally conceived."[33]

Troen's initial caution signaled by quotation marks when he first refers to "'Jewish' education" is resolved, there, in the State of Israel as a historical question: Can what is thought and taught to be Zionist identity subsume "Jewish" identity as it had been lived and articulated in Europe? The specter of the Shoah looms. With the destruction of European Jewry, its predominant model of Jewish identity could be consigned to the past. If Jewish identity was to survive in the Jewish State, it would do so in

Zionist terms. But Troen's comparative study of Israel and the United States reestablishes a coeval context, and with it another dimension of ethnic identity, namely, specification. Closely associated with Barth, anthropologist George Devereux condensed the specifying function to an Aristotelian formula, "A is an X . . . A is not a non-X."[34] But once coeval peoples are involved and mutual influence across the boundaries of ethnic identity is not only possible, but a common and constant feature of social life, the distinction between "is" and "is not" becomes difficult to maintain. Is an Israeli educated in the non-, if not anti-Zionist paradigm of American choice in no sense a non-X? Are an American who makes aliyah and an Israeli who settles in New York only the X they were to start with?

Responding critically to Barth, historian Shaye J. D. Cohen argues that ethnic boundaries do not represent an abstract structural principle, traced around a culture after the fact, but rather the boundaries are the permeable limits, always under construction, of what a given culture is able to recognize as its own.[35] Even where—even if—some cultural elements are unanimously accepted as pertaining to the ethnic identity, the boundaries are contested and negotiated terrain, with much traffic across the border in both directions. The relatively uncontested center is in a similar relationship with its own margins. Thus in investigating the ancient origins of "the inner mystery of Jewish identity or 'Jewishness,' the qualities that make a Jew a Jew,"[36] Cohen emphasizes the processes of cultural borrowing and the consequent cultural hybridization.

This interactive sociological model gives prominence to contextualization. Historian Amos Funkenstein deems the emergence of "a new *contextual* understanding" of the past a "revolution," which he dates to the early modern period between the sixteenth and eighteenth centuries,[37] in an argument that will be considered in some detail below. Here it suffices to note that the study of the concatenation of events, often presented as cause and effect, in the interest of establishing lines (more often a single line) of development, remained a mainstay of the historicism of the Science of Judaism. Contextualization is rather an effort to outline a setting, or various settings, in which events take on meaning. While it may be an old practice, as old as some versions of modernity, "contextualization" has become a key word in Jewish Studies and elsewhere, which speaks for a revised understanding of the task of the historian.

Understood as a matter of boundaries, ethnic (and sometimes personal) identity is necessarily a question of contextualization: ethnic boundaries circumscribe a context in themselves, and they are circumscribed in turn by larger contexts. In this light, identity shifts from an ontological and essentialist question of being—a Jew *is* an X, a Jew *is not* a non-X—to a matter of representation. Arendt had already focused attention on the Berlin open houses as a site for Jews to represent themselves; but as she and Rahel also knew, Jews are represented by others as well, and those representations form part of the context of Jewish identity. The essays collected by art historians Linda Nochlin and Tamar Garb under the title *The Jew in the Text* focus largely on antagonistic images, but they clarify issues in the construction of Jewish identity as a representation beyond the weak messianic task of putting antisemitism on trial. The Jew in the text is viewed as a certain kind of Jew—indeed may only be recognized as a Jew at all—in relation to particular "subtexts, contexts, and metatexts."[38] Nochlin, for instance, refers to the case of a lithograph by French Jewish artist Alphonse Lévy under the title "The Hebrew Lesson: The Portion" (1895), which was published in a special issue of a French journal dedicated to the World Zionist Congress of 1902, presumably as an objective or even positive image of the "the 'Jewish' world." The same image was later reprinted in a German collection of antisemitic caricatures in 1923.[39] Setting aside questions of positive and negative representations, the underlying point may be stated still more broadly: a boundary is not only a line of separation, but also an interface. No matter how far back one traces the beginnings of Jewishness, Jews will always be found to have had neighbors, who, in turn, have always had a voice in the determination, for any given now, of the "stuff"[40] enclosed by Jewish ethnic boundaries.

The movement of non-Jews and their representations of Jews across ethnic boundaries into the process of Jewish identity formation is paralleled by the outbound movement of Jews. On the one hand, Shaye Cohen recalls that in antiquity "to Judaize," from the Greek *ioudaïzein*, refers to gentiles passing as Jews.[41] On the other, historian Eric M. Meyers finds "synergy and syncretism" characteristic of Jewish life in Roman Palestine;[42] and historian Doron Mendels, generally cautious about such views, nevertheless recognizes that the Hasmonean state "was officially Jewish but had some Hellenist aspects."[43] In short, two-way traffic across a permeable boundary is not limited to the condition of Jewish modernity—unless, of course, a Golden Age of secure identity borders is assumed, thereby making permeability in itself the defining characteristic of modernity. But in those terms, Jews—and everybody else—will always have been modern, and Cohen can close his discussion of the beginnings of Jewish identity by asserting that "our post-rabbinic world mirrors the pre-rabbinic world of antiquity."[44]

An Ashkenazi-centric Jewish Studies has tended to make the assumption of a bounded, separate Jewish sphere in relative, if not absolute terms, often judging modern conditions of admixture in any age as an exile from the Garden. Scholar of modern Yiddish and Hebrew literature

David G. Roskies illustrates those Ashkenazic boundaries by comparing the fictional character Tevye the milkman, now familiar worldwide as the hero of *Fiddler on the Roof*, to the real life of Solomon Rabinovitsch, the author who created him in a series of Yiddish stories, writing under the well-known pseudonym Sholom Aleichem. Tevye lived in a setting in which "everything a Jew needed to know about the world was locatable in [a virtual] Universal Jewish Encyclopedia," and Roskies is able to reconstruct the abridged table of contents of the "sum total of [Tevye's] book learning" drawn from those sources.[45] The author was a resident of the burgeoning city of late nineteenth-century Kiev and a reader of much non-Jewish European literature, which provided the basis for his conception of the modern genres of the short story and the novel. Rabinovitsch "no longer had any truck with Jewish covenantal memory," writes Roskies,[46] yet he created a character who was bounded by the canonical reading list that describes and transmits the covenant, and thereby mapped a Jewish *world* of Sholem Aleichem, in the words of Maurice Samuel.[47]

The trope of a separate Jewish world is a mainstay of Ashkenazic studies. Yet the force of the underlying thesis that the Jewishness of a Jewish identity is that which is separable from admixture and bounded by a canon, variously defined and often only implied, extends into other areas in Jewish Studies as well. In a formula that is but a more extreme version of Roskies's depiction of Rabinovitsch as a modern author, for instance, historian Renée Levine Malammed suggests that over the course of generations, Iberian conversos "had no Jewish memory to speak of."[48] The emphasis falls on the absolute absence of both any fulfillment of covenantal obligations and any knowledge of the forbidden books in which those obligations were defined; but the implication is that recollection of converso experience, which would have been available over the course of those generations, does not itself constitute "Jewish memory." Against that negation, Malammed immediately adds that nevertheless "there is a Jewish aspect to their ethnic identity that differentiates them from the Iberian nonconversos,"[49] which is the real burden of her argument. The point may be broadened: as a key word in the current state of Jewish Studies, identity is most often a conceptual gathering point for non-canonical elements of knowledge and practice, which may still serve the purposes of differentiating and therefore specifying Jews.

Studying Jews who pass into, pass through (recalling Jaspers), or pass in the social worlds beyond their own ethnic boundaries presents a challenge to such a deployment of identity. Historian Derek J. Penslar illustrates the difficulties in his discussion of "Jewish economics" with regard to a seventeenth-century text published in Spanish in Amsterdam,

*Confusion of Confusions*, by Joseph Penso de la Vega. Penslar remarks that "nothing about the book's format or content is overtly Jewish, although the writing does have certain classic Marrano characteristics, such as the heavy use of imagery from the Old Testament and classical antiquity while shying away from any Christian references."[50] But the absence of Christian contents does not yet make for the presence of a specifying Jewish identification. Both the Hebrew Scriptures as Old Testament and Greco-Roman antiquity would also have been available to "Christian economics." So, Penslar continues, "only an antisemite could find anything 'Jewish' about de la Vega's economic sensibilities, which simply reflect those of any prudent investor trying to turn a profit in the hectic world of the securities market in the late seventeenth century."[51] Penslar's cautionary quotation marks around "Jewish" in this passage defend against an essentialist understanding of identity. Only in an antisemitic context can "investor," prudent or not, be equated with "Jew" and "Jew" with "investor" (capitalist, usurer, etc.). Essentialisms are all but invariably forms of ideological oppression, because they eliminate free will in favor of some ontological or biological determinism. The hypothetical antisemitic readers work backward in a confusion of confusions of their own. The text does not include specifying Jewish features in Penslar's analysis; the Jewishness of de la Vega's economics is only inferred from the implied intertext of his biography. The Jewish identity of the text lies outside the text—in its contexts or the potential antisemitic subtexts of some of its readers. And yet Penslar himself includes *Confusion of Confusions* in his economic history of Jewish identity.

What Penslar refers to as "the conceptual and methodological problem of whether there is anything *intrinsically* Jewish about a text penned by a Jew but lacking any overt Jewish *content*"[52] is currently being addressed by questioning the notion of the "intrinsic," the function of boundaries, and the role of contents, through a revision of theories of identity. Most notably, a theory of multiple subject positions makes it possible to conceive of identity as a conglomerate of disparate elements, simultaneously present, but differentially active. One may be a Jew *and* an investor. In that case, investing is not intrinsically Jewish, nor is Jewishness defined by investing. But since the Jewish investor is both a Jew and an investor at once, the points of intersection make for a rich area of research. Intellectual historian Martin Jay moves cautiously to that area in studying the Jews who established the Institute of Social Research in Frankfurt in the 1920s, and then reestablished it as refugees in New York: "Even the most assimilated Jews in Wilhelmine Germany *must have felt* somewhat apart from their gentile counterparts," a bitter experience "which *might easily feed* a radical critique of the society as a whole"—with emphasis added to underline Jay's agnosticism on this point. Jay continues, "This is not to say that the Institut's program can be solely, or even predominantly, attributed to its members' ethnic roots, but merely to argue that to ignore them entirely is to lose sight of one contributing factor."[53]

A bolder argument is made possible, however, by a view of identity as the interaction of various subject positions within the same individual or group. The very logic of sameness is thus opened to question. As Marla Brettschneider argues, Jews have canonically represented themselves otherwise in any case,[54] and this mode provides the grounds for a specific contribution that Jewish Studies can make to other, related fields. Or, as scholar of religious studies Barbara A. Holdredge states: "What does an exploration of the intersections of Indic and Judaic cultures contribute to the broader scholarly enterprise of religious studies and the human sciences more generally? . . . A method of critical interrogation that can serve as a means to dismantle the tyranny of prevailing paradigms and to construct a range of alternative epistemologies."[55]

The publication history of Brettschneider's essay is noteworthy in this regard. Originally appearing in a collection devoted strictly to studying Jews, it has since been reprinted, crossing over to a more general collection on feminist politics.[56] Literary critic Sara Horowitz's plaint at the excision of Jewish Studies from the cohort of ethnic studies that had grown together in the wake of the politicizing of the curriculum in the 1960s was well taken when she first said, "Gettin' mighty lonely out here," in 1994.[57] It would still describe an isolation little changed a decade and a half later. But the isolation is not simply the result of antagonistic forces, much as these have been realigned and reinforced as a result of the Israeli occupation of territories gained in the Six Day War of 1967. Focus on identity had previously often served to reinforce Jewish ethnic boundaries from within as the task of Jewish Studies. Brettschneider's deconstruction of identity is exemplary of more recent trends in the field, and the reprinting in *Feminist Politics* gives evidence that as an avenue to reenter conversation with what Horowitz called the "natural allies" of Jewish Studies, such a contestation of the logic of identity has willing partners. Furthermore, making difference, rather than sameness, the basis for discussion enlarges the conversation within Jewish Studies as well, manifested, for instance, by Brettschneider, drawing upon the work of feminist and queer theorist Melanie Kaye/Kantrowitz.[58] For even in those areas of Jewish life where women are still treated as children of a lesser god, to live as a woman is not a sin, whereas most homosexual practice is considered to be so, as Sandi Simcha Dubowski explores in the documentary film *Trembling Before G-d*.[59]

A remark by a foundational figure for Jewish feminist theology, Rabbi Rachel Adler, writing in a different context, makes for an apt introduction to Brettschneider's theoretical position:

> But a tradition cannot be reduced to a shelf of books or an argument. It is a way groups of people live out stories and arguments in relationships, in ritual, in play, in work, and in love. Feminist adherents to traditional faith and feminists of color may question [the] bland assumption that gender, all by itself, can provide a tradition, a language, a basis for shared understandings that transcends and replaces the bonds of religious and cultural heritages preserved in collective memories. . . . As a Jew, I ask, what is it that should impel me to turn away from the seder table saying, "That has nothing to do with me," and say instead to Mary Wollstonecraft and Doris Lessing, "You are my people and my heritage"?[60]

One notes Adler's plural and mixed "heritages" in contrast to the insistence on a singular, and thus pure, feminist legacy. Adler lays claim simultaneously to identity positions as a woman and a Jew, and thus to an intellectual base in both Jewish Studies and Women's Studies.

As Brettschneider points out, feminist theory itself has promoted the premise of multiplicity. She begins in praise of "mutual constitution theory in feminist philosophy,"[61] that is, a mode of social analysis in which several different factors are understood to interact with one another inseparably. An analysis of class devoid of considerations of race (typical of classical Marxism, for instance), or the reverse, the study of race without reference to class, would fail on the grounds of reductionism. She offers as an example of this salutary trend in feminist theory philosopher Elizabeth V. Spelman's *Inessential Woman*:

> According to Spelman, we often find ourselves and our political commentators asking about the status of women and Blacks in the military. She reminds us that such a statement actually makes no sense, since some women in the military are Black and some Blacks are also women. Not only is this faulty language used, but given the racist biases in gender analysis and the sexist biases in race-based analysis, the category 'Black' is taken to mean Blacks who are not women. This structure leaves out an important group of human beings: Black women.[62]

Yet, while appreciative of Spelman's achievement, Brettschneider notes a collapse in her mutually constitutive approach that is the direct result, in Brettschneider's view, of the "translat[ion] of the ancient Greek notion of slave into the modern idiom of race."[63]

Brettschneider makes clear that she learns from Spelman and other theorists of race, class, and gender differences to attend to power relations *within* Jewish social organization, as is particularly clear in her discussion of Jewish lesbianism. So, too, in his investigation of the *mensch* as "femminized male," Daniel Boyarin remains wary of idealizations. Relative to the surrounding, hegemonic culture, Jewish masculinity may represent an alternative to the violence of the various Knights of the Burning Pestle, but, Boyarin admonishes, "we do not have . . . a pure celebration of femaleness, not by any means."[64] For the "femminized male" is as hegemonic within the traditional Jewish social order as the manly male is in the surrounding culture. The pen of the male domain of Jewish learning is as mighty as the Crusader's sword in at least one respect: the power it allows Jewish men to wield over Jewish women.

Nevertheless, the dialogue between Jewish Studies and the study of other differences remains two-sided. Brettschneider points out that in adopting Aristotle's discussion of slaves as a theoretical foundation, Spelman also incorporates his gender blindness. From this critical observation, Brettschneider goes on to contest the Aristotelian logic of the either/or, by presenting the alternative logic of a talmudic construction of overlapping categories. Her proposal of a distinctively Jewish logic is reinforced by Marvin Fox's reading of Maimonides, that most Aristotelian of Jewish thinkers. Studying the *Guide of the Perplexed* in light of both medieval and modern critiques of its puzzling contradictions, Fox claims that Maimonides' approach to certain paradoxes "is to eschew the way of 'either/or' and to adopt instead the way of 'both/and.'"[65] He details Maimonides' introduction and deployment of a new term, "divergences," outside of the technical Aristotelian vocabulary ("contradictions" and "contraries") that he received from medieval Arabic sources.[66] To understand the "divergences from the truth," Fox explains, one must have recourse to a dictum from Maimonides' Introduction to the *Guide*: "In speaking about very obscure matters it is necessary to conceal some parts and to disclose others."[67] The divergences are signposts to the reader.

Brettschneider's emphasis in her reading of the talmudic alternative to Aristotelian non-contradiction falls on its implications for the understanding of power. "What one finds is that the difference between Spelman's Aristotle and the Talmudic text is not simply that there are more classifications and groups named [in the latter]," writes Brettschneider, "but that the internal logic of the Talmudic text challenges its own named categories as discrete and separable entities and makes it impossible to develop a linear presentation of power relationships at all, let alone one that is stable or fixed."[68] She concludes that the "hegemonic texts" of the Western academy, even at their most critical, reinforce foundational power relationships. One cannot tear down the master's house using Aristotle's tools, to paraphrase poet and essayist Audre Lorde.

Thus, Brettschneider urges that feminist theorists and others working in the politicized curriculum that is ours since the 1960s may do well to turn to "Jewish texts as countertexts,"[69] which resist the reduction of multiple social markers to binary pairs. Reading the Talmud as *both* canon *and* counter reopens the boundaries of identity to the conversation of differences. Even the Talmud may be studied as well as learned.

## Building Memories

Education is the principal arena of social reproduction, which, French sociologist Pierre Bourdieu argued, generally means the reinforcement of existing social hierarchies.[70] As a field in the setting of nonsectarian institutions of higher learning, Jewish Studies is charged with the reproduction of "Europe" (to continue to employ Chakrabarty's quotation marks): to inculcate the value of the individuated self as the locus of free will, expressed through critical thinking, for instance, and the related valorization of certain kinds of individuals whose positions within structures of power allow them to exercise agency and voice. The institutions of Jewish learning reproduce Jewish values—fulfillment of the covenantal obligations revealed at Sinai, above all—and authorize some members of the covenantal community to interpret the obligations and oversee their fulfillment. Yet for all the distinctions between the social contexts and goals of these two forms of education, there are also areas of overlap between them, much as Maimonides, Fox, and Brettschneider suggest— not least the tendency to privilege the same social subset of heterosexual males from certain parts of Europe (north of the Mediterranean coastal area) and their descendants.

The educational institutions of Jewish learning and Jewish Studies can sometimes serve one another's goals of social reproduction. Scholar of the Kabbalah Moshe Idel relates, for example, that "now, for the first time, academicians can not only learn from [contemporary, practicing] Kabbalists and their works but also help them by providing information on manuscripts or biographical data on Kabbalists that would otherwise be inaccessible to them."[71] And almost any instructor in a Jewish Studies classroom will be familiar with many students who are not studying Jews as an external object, as *them*, but rather as *us*, seeking points of contact between their own lives and other Jewish experiences as the basis for grounding their sense of their own Jewish identity—just as, say, the English major in an American university, though the connection is so common and so fundamental to the institution as to go unnoticed.

Historian Steven J. Zipperstein relates a converse situation in his discussion of the surprisingly broad support in turn-of-the-twentieth-century Russia for the institution of the *heder*, that is, the traditional Eastern

European, Jewish primary school. Despite fierce opposition on most issues, Zionists and Integrationists joined in their advocacy of the *heder*. Political parties with antagonistic visions of the terms by which Jews should negotiate their entrance into modernity, but sharing their rejection of a certain Jewish past, nevertheless turned to a traditional institution of social reproduction as a means toward social revolution. "It was anxiety that inspired them," explains Zipperstein, "an unease, sometimes expressed openly (though generally taken for granted), that Jewish youth were slipping away from things Jewish and that the disappearance of the heder would immeasurably worsen this situation."[72] Zionists pressed for a Jewish nation-state as the political status appropriate to modern Jews, while Integrationists saw Jewish political modernity as a matter of equality as citizens in any state. But they found common ground in identity: let modern Jews be Jewish. Where ethnic identity was threatened, the *heder* offered an educational setting for the reinforcement of group boundaries (e.g., separate schooling) and of the mechanisms of mutual recognition within those boundaries (e.g., sharing an ethnically marked language through instruction in Hebrew).

Zipperstein points to a methodological problem in his account of Jewish ethnic identity as it was manifest in the movement to reform but preserve the *heder*: "What tended to enter the historical record (in Russia, perhaps, more so than elsewhere in modern Jewish life) was often the product of the most ideologically coherent groups . . . who tended to airbrush their antagonists from the past with the sincerity, cunning, or innocence of political conviction."[73] His qualification, "more so than elsewhere," might be easily overturned and his concerns augmented. In Russia, as elsewhere, and not only in modern times, there are peoples without history—that is, without access to the record that counts as history. And among them, there are Jews without history, as there are peoples who identify themselves as Jews who are denied the sanction of mutual recognition, and airbrushed, as it were, from "the" history of "the" Jews. Those who are only representing themselves, without the reverberation of mutual recognition, may well affirm personal identity without achieving ethnic identity. Zipperstein frames the methodological problem, and the underlying political issues, by setting forth the current terms in which they are debated in Jewish Studies in the subtitle of his lecture series: memory, history, identity. The study of identity has witnessed a shift from a foundation in history, dating back to the inaugural period of modern Jewish Studies, to a new emphasis on memory.

Like identity, memory is most pertinent to Jewish Studies inasmuch as it can be constructed as a social rather than a personal process. Currently, the all but inevitable point of reference is *The Social Frameworks of Memory*, the work of French sociologist Maurice Halbwachs, a Catholic who died in the Buchenwald concentration camp as a result of having investigated and protested the murders of his Jewish wife and her parents by the authorities, whether French or German, in occupied France.[74] As above with Bynum's delineation of identity theories, the interests of dialogue with allied fields will be served by turning to Egyptologist Jan Assmann for a succinct summary of Halbwachs's conception of collective memory:

> For Halbwachs, memory is developed in individuals in proportion to their communication with others and their membership of social constellations. In the absence of such membership and communication, the individual is unable to organize his internal images and shape them as memories. Memory is a parameter of social organization. . . . This social parameter is transmitted to the individual through his association with other people, and it introduces structure into his chaotic inner life. . . . For Halbwachs the past is not an objective given, but a collective reconstruction.[75]

The collectivity reconstructs the past and in so doing it also reconstructs itself as the heir of a particular legacy. History marks turning points and more revolutionary ruptures. Collective memory asserts continuity. And remembering, in this sociological view, is simultaneously re-membering, signing up ever anew as a member of the collectivity, laying claim to mutual recognition, identifying. To study Jewish ethnic identity through the formulations and manifestations of Jewish memory is a response to the imperative of survival where and when continuity is threatened and membership in the collectivity of Jews has been decimated.

Drawing directly on Halbwachs, historian Yosef Hayim Yerushalmi has provided an articulation of the concept of Jewish collective memory in a series of lectures, published as *Zakhor: Jewish History and Jewish Memory*, one of the most influential books in the current state of the question.[76] The exemplary expression of Jewish memory, for Yerushalmi, is the Passover Haggadah, with its talmudic injunction: "In each and every generation let all persons regard themselves as though they each had emerged from Egypt," to adapt his translation. "For whatever memories were unleashed by the commemorative rituals and liturgies were surely not a matter of intellection," writes Yerushalmi, "but of evocation and identification. There are sufficient clues to indicate that what was suddenly drawn up from the past was not a series of facts to be contemplated at a distance, but a series of situations into which one could somehow be existentially drawn."[77]

The shaping force of *Zakhor* goes beyond particular analyses. Yerushalmi would renegotiate the pedagogical contract between Jewish

Studies and the contemporary academy by asserting that critical historiography is alien to Jewish learning and, conversely, that the traditional,
participatory modes of Jewish memory offer an alternative paradigm for
studying Jews in their own terms. "History" is "Europe," in this argument, and studying Jews historically leads inevitably to the reproduction
of "Europe" at the expense of Jewish identity. Like Brettschneider in relation to the Talmud, one might look to (instead of looking at) the texts of
Jewish learning as resources for modes of studying Jews Jewishly.

Historian David N. Myers has underlined that *Zakhor* is an outgrowth
of Yerushalmi's previous research studying Sephardic Jews.[78] The
Marrano context had given Yerushalmi occasion to consider peoples who
had often been airbrushed from history by social hierarchies on both
the Jewish and non-Jewish sides of their complex hybrid identities.
Yerushalmi had stated, "If we are to perceive the meaning of Marranism
in the twentieth century, we must not approach the problem with pre-
conceived notions as to what constitutes 'Jewishness' nor, least of all,
with legalistic definitions." He continues, "Rather than superimpose
external criteria which derive from traditional Jewish life and behavior,
thereby ignoring the genuine peculiarities of the Converso position, we
should try to confine ourselves to an inductive method."[79] An inductive
method would elucidate internal criteria: Marrano voices speaking for
their own understanding of Marrano life and behavior. And to hear those
voices requires an expansion of what Zipperstein calls "the historical
record," which he situates at the point of collusion between knowledge
and power. If the Marranos do not write themselves into Jewish history,
it would nonetheless be possible to hear their voices as Jewish memories.

The inductive method that Yerushalmi advocated in studying
Marranos proves equally applicable to "traditional Jewish life and behavior." Moreover, studying Sephardim more generally opens the imperative
of survival to the considerations of the *longue durée*. The "both/and" com-
plexion of Sephardic experience, especially notable in the extreme
instance of the Marranos, has proven to be a successful mode of survival,
and not a posthumous victory for Ferdinand and Isabella. These two
points—the practices of memory as a Jewish alternative to history as well
as the both/and conception of Jewish identity—are especially well illustrated in studying Jews outside of "Europe" and the Ashkenazic center of
Jewish Studies.

Yerushalmi draws attention to Gerson D. Cohen's work on the *Sefer
Ha-Qabbalah* or *Book of Tradition*, by Abraham Ibn Daud, a twelfth-century
Jewish philosopher from Muslim al-Andalus.[80] Cohen was a historian, a
faculty member at Columbia University at the time that Yerushalmi studied there, and eventually chancellor of the Jewish Theological Seminary

in New York. Along with preparing a critical edition of Ibn Daud's Hebrew text and an English translation, a historical introduction and a substantial textual analysis, he was also an embodiment of the "both/ and": both a staunch Zionist from a Hebrew-speaking American household and the author of "The Blessing of Assimilation."[81]

Ibn Daud presents a history of an unbroken Jewish teaching tradition stretching from biblical times to his own contemporary al-Andalus. With this book in hand, one might expect to support the consensual view of the formation of Jewish Studies as the advent of a secularizing historiography and simply displace the point of departure from Berlin to Iberian Toledo, while setting the clock back to the Middle Ages. Cohen, however, marks that historical line at two moments of significant discontinuity. First and foremost, he points to the frustration of modern scholars in their attempts to assimilate the *Sefer ha-Qabbalah* into the tradition of the new. Cohen himself outlines the problem in arithmetic terms, which are paradigmatic for the post-Enlightenment emphasis on rationality (grounded etymologically in the Latin for counting, calculating, and reckoning). Referring to Ibn Daud's dates, by the Jewish calendar, for various periods, figures, and events, Cohen writes: "What is one to make of a statement, repeated for emphasis, that $62 \times 7 = 420$! Or that $4449 - 187 = 4260$! Or that $4798 - 13 = 4775$!"[82]

The arithmetical problem "troubled modern scholars," Cohen remarks.[83] In this regard he cites Science of Judaism scholar S.J.L. Rapoport, who proposed in 1839 that Ibn Daud's primary source for the history of the talmudic and gaonic periods was a particular tenth-century document, the *Epistle* of Sherira Gaon. According to Rapoport, "Ibn Daud's mistake on the places of service of [three] generations of geonim, could be easily accounted for by assuming that in the text of the Epistle which he consulted, the name Sura had been omitted in one spot. This error in his source caused Ibn Daud *to compound error upon error*, in view of the requirement he felt to square the limits of Sherira's chronology with his own."[84]

The main thrust of Cohen's historical argument is to provincialize the work of such scholarship in the Science of Judaism mold, which had adopted the universalizing standards of "Europe." Contextualizing Ibn Daud firmly in his local intellectual environment, Cohen views the twelfth-century *Sefer ha-Qabbalah* as a polemical work, meeting the challenge of a Karaite movement resurgent in medieval Iberia. The weak flank of Karaism—a movement that identified itself as Jewish but rejected the Oral Torah as true revelation, and hence the authority of the rabbis and their Talmud—appeared to be its relative modernity. For in Ibn Daud's milieu, the Karaite movement was dated no further back than the ninth century. The authority of rabbinic Judaism derived from its greater antiquity, founded upon the claims of *continuous* transmission by worthy masters to worthy students, which is precisely what Ibn Daud sought to attest. Projecting his standards backward, Rapoport expected to find a precursor to the Science of Judaism. Anticipating Yerushalmi, Cohen demonstrates instead that taken in the sense theorized and practiced by the Science of Judaism, Ibn Daud was no historian.

Cohen himself will only wear the disciplinary legacy with a difference. "The discovery of sources for every single statement in *Sefer ha-Qabbalah* will not account for the method and intent of the author," Cohen asserts. "These can be elicited and determined only by examining the work as a unit and as the product of a man who wished to say something that for reasons of his own he did not immediately make obvious to his reading public."[85] Cohen stakes his historical method to the philosophical procedures of phenomenology, grounded in the work of German Jewish philosopher Edmund Husserl. He discerns the "method and intent" of Ibn Daud through what Idel, in another self-consciously phenomenological approach within Jewish Studies, calls the "organization of knowledge."[86] The significant dates in *Sefer ha-Qabbalah*, Cohen argues, are organized symmetrically, rather than as a strict chronological succession: "If Ibn Daud's periodization of history has been a problem, it is because scholars have sought respectable literary sources and rational criteria to account for the vagaries of a man who never felt bound by such canons."[87] Those historicist scholars have been distracted by source criticism, prejudiced by their own faith in rationality, and, above all, misguided by "prescriptive statements"[88] concerning the nature of history.

Once historicist assumptions are set aside, the equal sign of rational arithmetic becomes the symmetrical sign of divine intervention. In the *Sefer ha-Qabbalah*, Cohen concludes, "History is a kind of sermon, a medium of insight into the workings of Providence, and, accordingly, a vehicle of solace for Israel."[89] So rather than fault Ibn Daud for failing to achieve what he did not intend, namely, a rationalized, historical account, Cohen brings forth a distinct intention, a traditional Jewish mode of organizing knowledge in the framework of the covenantal relationship: Jewish learning on the one side, the messianic promise on the other. In that light, Cohen rediscovers Ibn Daud as a starting point for modern Jewish Studies, not because he anticipates the mode of studying Jews historically of the Science of Judaism, but because he metaphorized religious discourse in the apparently—but only apparently—secular mold of historiography.

Memory provides the alternative to history as a scientific discipline in Cohen's reading of the *Sefer ha-Qabbalah* as a Rabbanite defense against the pressures of Karaite rebellion. Rabbinic authority is founded upon the claim to a participatory relationship to the past. The Karaites contest rabbinic memory from within the Jewish community—the authority of the Sinai revelation as written in the Torah is not in doubt—but speaking on behalf of the Rabbanites, Ibn Daud finds support across the border of the religious and ethnic divide of al-Andalus. Cohen comments, "That the 'chain' of succession which [Ibn Daud] described was one of sanctity untainted by interruption or hiatus, has a familiar ring to students of Islam, in which . . . 'verified' and 'concatenated' attestations have the same purpose and weight."[90] From this Cohen concludes, much as Américo Castro might have understood, though in a direction Castro himself did not investigate, "in his very choice of terms as well as of concepts, Ibn Daud—and of course, all others who used such terms—hoped to convince an audience that had absorbed the basic premises and vocabulary of Arabic scholarship."[91] In short, Ibn Daud spoke in the idiom of his culturally mixed Iberian *dwelling place*, drawing on non-Jewish resources to reinforce a Jewish position in an intra-communal polemic. Ibn Daud's "sermon" was both Jewish and Andalusian.

This point, crucial to Yerushalmi's understanding of Jewish memory in *Zakhor*, is the cornerstone of one of the great achievements of scholarship in Jewish Studies in the current period, historian S. D. Goitein's multi-volume study of the late medieval period, *A Mediterranean Society: The Jewish Communities of the Arab World*.[92] It is possible to situate Goitein himself in a memory tradition of direct transmission. He was born in Germany in 1900 in an Orthodox milieu and received his university training at Frankfurt in philology, a disciplinary mainstay of the Science of Judaism, and, more particularly, as an "orientalist," which was the corner of the curriculum left over for studying Jews when Jewish Studies itself was still without academic standing in Europe (with or without quotation marks). In addition, Goitein had close contact with Franz Rosenzweig at Frankfurt, and so exposure to his transformative enactment of Jewish learning. He then made aliyah, joining Gershom Scholem among the inaugural faculty of the Hebrew University.

Goitein eventually settled at Princeton University in the United States, where he published the first volume of *A Mediterranean Society* in 1967, the same year as Cohen's edition of *Sefer ha-Qabbalah*. A direct link to the Wissenschaft movement, Goitein is nonetheless an exemplary figure for the new curriculum of the 1960s, dedicated to reconstructing the history of peoples without history. His descriptive, "sociographic" approach to the medieval history of Jews in lands under Muslim rule expanded the historical record and deliberately eschewed the prejudgments of "Europe" in favor of giving voice to the value judgments "made from the point of view of the actors on the scene."[93]

Goitein accomplished his task by concentrating research on the literal debris of history. He worked on a very particular set of texts, namely the vast and varied resources of the Cairo Geniza. The collection includes hundreds of thousands of discarded documents, preserved for centuries in the attic of a Cairo synagogue due to the prohibition against destroying objects bearing the name of God. A large portion of the texts were studied, collected, and transferred to Cambridge, beginning in 1896, by Rabbi Solomon Schechter, Romanian born and educated in Germany, but already a prominent scholar in England at the time, and later the president of the Jewish Theological Seminary in New York and a major figure in the Conservative movement in America. The transfer of documents and other archeological treasures from colonized areas to metropolitan centers might raise questions now that seem not to have concerned earlier scholars in the field.

Goitein inverted the hierarchy of the documents. Where Schechter and others focused on variant versions of classical texts in the Cairo Geniza, especially autograph manuscripts of major figures, with a primary interest in religious studies, Goitein devoted himself to mundane records of daily life, above all commercial documents, with an eye toward material culture. Goitein reconstructs, again quite literally, the dwelling place of medieval Jews in the Mediterranean basin living chiefly under Muslim rule.

In practice, this means, for instance, setting aside ideological predispositions that frame the home as the site of the same people living in the same place. Detailing an arrangement wherein partners in the ownership of a dwelling share "the amenities of the best section of a house" by rotating, "year by year from one floor, or one part of the house to the other," Goitein withdraws from judgment: "Strange as the arrangement may appear to us, it shows how much care was taken to avoid squabbles between members of a family who were joint owners of a house."[94] It further shows that the "tension between . . . two opposing tendencies of family cohesion and mobility"[95] was not marked in material culture by a division between the Jew in the home and the person on the street, but rather was lived out in a dwelling in which mobility was as internalized as cohesion. Nor was cohesion absent outside the home. Hence, in explicit contrast to "the countries that most typify Judeo-Christian confrontations in medieval Europe,"[96] Goitein characterizes the Jewish environment in the medieval Arab world as one of constant transaction: "Partnerships with outsiders, even members of another religion, were common."[97] Goitein relates the partnerships—with both insiders and outsiders—as microhistories of the dwelling places themselves, which is to say that he is studying Jews without confining himself to the dichotomy of agency and passivity. Neither resisters, nor victims, nor collaborators in their own demise, Goitein represents Jews as partners: an alternative response to the imperative of survival.

The homey dimensions of material culture brought to the fore by Goitein combine with the participatory element of memory underlined by Yerushalmi to form the basis of much research in the current state of Jewish Studies and indeed a characteristic note in the Jewish Studies classroom—implicitly in the university setting, and explicitly in the extramural venues of adult education in synagogue reading groups, *havuroth*, and Jewish Community Centers. The Jewish Science of the nineteenth century and its later avatars were built on a cornerstone of neutral, critical distance: a strict (though strictly ideal) separation of the subject of research, that is, the researcher, from the object of study. The politicized curriculum emerging in the 1960s questioned both the possibility and the desirability of that neutrality, arguing on democratic and demographic grounds for broader representation. Unless learning is misconstrued as abetting one's own subjugation, one cannot learn where one finds no reflection in one's educational institutions. The insistence on representing Jews and other marginalized constituencies of the university in the curriculum is not simply politically correct; it is pedagogically correct. Jews studying Jews, and therefore themselves, is sometimes written off as a narcissistic "identity politics," but in an era grown acutely conscious of the collusion of knowledge and power, largely through the work of French thinker Michel Foucault, that self-reflection is a true political stance: re-membering is a form of empowerment.

A memory discipline, anthropology plays an important role in the current state of Jewish Studies, which had been initiated primarily within the field of history. Anthropology developed as a modern discipline, especially under the direction of French Jewish foundational figure Emile Durkheim around the turn of the twentieth century, on the basis of field research by participant-observers. The anthropologist was to be an outsider, but in the midst of the insiders: a privileged location for eyewitness testimony and holistic accounts. A century later, a more self-reflexive ethnography has problematized the "scientific" distance between researcher and object of study.[98] The prejudices of the researcher, including the valorization of anthropology as a scientific discipline, are now generally acknowledged as crucial data of ethnographies because they obscure "the point of view of the *other* actors on the scene" (to vary Goitein's formulation). Where Jewish researchers are studying Jews the distinction of insiders and outsiders is further effaced: psychotherapist Marc Kaminsky conducts his field research at his grandmother's kitchen table, reconstructing her memories of emigration and immigration; Ruth Behar theorizes and practices the role of the "vulnerable observer" of her Cuban Jewish background; Jonathan Boyarin re-members, that is, reinscribes himself as a member, of his own minyan at Manhattan's Eighth Street shul.[99]

The impact of the paradigm of memory and the context of the material dwelling place on the current state of Jewish Studies may be best illustrated by considering explicitly an interdisciplinary dialogue with history. Three texts representing generational and gender differences and focusing on widely dispersed *lieux de mémoire* (memory sites)[100] may serve the purpose: Irving Howe's *World of Our Fathers* (1976), Anita Shapira's *Land and Power* (1992), and Joëlle Bahloul's *The Architecture of Memory* (1992).[101]

Separated by two generations, Howe and Bahloul are both children of Jewish immigrants, the former born on New York's Lower East Side and raised in the Bronx, the latter born in France in a family of Algerian Jewish émigrés. Shapira, positioned generationally between Howe and Bahloul, was born in Poland at the outset of World War II but educated in Israel. Like Howe, Shapira has demonstrated a longstanding interest in left-wing politics, but she is closer to Bahloul in professional formation, in that both women received clearly delineated disciplinary training leading to doctorates in their fields: Shapira in history and Bahloul in anthropology. Howe, on the other hand, rose to prominence outside the academy, forming part of the mid-twentieth-century group, mostly Jewish, widely known as "the New York Intellectuals," and associated with the *Partisan Review*, *Commentary*, and *Dissent* (which Howe co-founded). His writing is correspondingly more eclectic with regard to discipline, moving between social and political history, cultural criticism, and, above all, literary studies. Shapira and Bahloul are also closer to one another insofar as both have devoted their professional lives to studying Jews, whereas Howe did not. Raised in a Yiddish-speaking milieu, Howe had co-edited, with Eliezer Greenberg, *A Treasury of Yiddish Stories*, an important collection in translation as early as 1954, followed more than a decade later by *A Treasury of Yiddish Poetry*.[102] Nevertheless, as a large-scale writing project of his own in the field of Jewish Studies, *World of Our Fathers* marks a significant departure from his previous work.

When one considers the documents produced in evidence of *World of Our Fathers* and *Land and Power*, one finds that both Howe and Shapira have broadened the historical record to include various forms of personal testimony, notably memoirs in Howe's case and poetry in Shapira's. Yet despite his work in literary studies, Howe remains oddly reticent about interpreting the myriad texts he adduces. They stand as corroboration of his account, conceived in a historicist sense as "an accurate record."[103] He follows the stages of emigration as model structures, rather than individuated events, in keeping with the methods of social history.

The texts of memories that Howe invokes, therefore, give a sense of the range of typical experience. Early in the narrative, Howe verges on a different approach than verification: "Was the Atlantic crossing really as dreadful as memoirists and legend have made it out to be?" He adds, "One thing seems certain: to have asked such questions of a representative portion of Jews who came to America between 1881 and 1914 would have elicited stares of disbelief, suspicions as to motive, perhaps worse. The imagery of the journey as ordeal was deeply imprinted in the Jewish folk-mind—admittedly, a mind with a rich training in the imagery of ordeal."[104] The misrecognition that Howe attributes to the respondents is neither a matter of fact nor an answer to his question, but rather a hypothetical construction, for lack of textual evidence. Howe finds himself obliged to admit, as a kind of addendum, that the imprint of the imagery of ordeal preceded the experience of the Atlantic crossing that the folk-mind purportedly recorded.

The "Jewish folk-mind" may be best understood as what Halbwachs theorized as a social framework of memory as applied to the Eastern European Jews who came to the United States via the infamous steerage. Because their collective memory already included the motif of ordeal as a prominent element, individuals remembered with special vividness the crossing as an ordeal. Or to put this otherwise, suffering and surviving ordeals were vital elements in the collective identity of these Jews when they were still in Europe, and the recollection of the crossing as an ordeal was a process of re-membering. By representing their new experience as a metaphorization of the grueling experiences of old, they reaffirmed both their ties to their forebears and to their new cohort. But this is not the general direction of Howe's study.

Instead, Howe usually turns to the memoirs much as he does when drawing on the evidence of bureaucratic records. His purpose is to contest the "legend" or collective memory of Jewish immigration in the name of history. Thus, looking at census information, Howe finds that "the number of young people on [Rivington and Madison Streets] working in white-collar occupations is notably higher than on Cherry Street." He then adds, programmatically, "Again, however, *no evidence can be found for the commonly held notion* that there occurs a sudden and massive ascent of the children of immigrants to professional and middle-class status."[105] Memoirs are trumped by "objective" documents; their historical value is limited to the advantages they hold for narrative as personalized, and hence, vivid illustrations of the evidence that can be found in other forms, such as statistical information. But if, for Howe, the memoirs cannot be assimilated to the historical record without further corroboration, he does not generally consider their contribution to the register of collective memory. He does not ask which social frameworks are evidenced by individual memoirs.

Such a question, on the other hand, might well articulate the fundamental goal of Shapira, the historian, who is less bound by historicist premises than Howe. Writing about the "myth of Tel Hai" of 1920, which grew from an armed clash between that settlement in northern Palestine and a nearby Arab village, resulting in the death of six Jewish settlers, among them the prominent figure Joseph Trumpeldor, she states:

> What interests us are the psychological and public needs that generated a certain story in public imagination and transformed it into something larger than life, giving it a special, almost transcendental meaning. The messages and symbols the myth communicates seem to us far more important than the question, What is the factual core of the story, and what is the mythic sheath in which it is enveloped? The messages and symbols are bound up with an additional question, namely, Why did a special myth emerge at a certain place and time?[106]

The emphasis on the particularities of time and place mark the historian's concern, but in the bracketing of facticity, Shapira declares this to be a study of collective memory. What social framework existing at that moment—and long after, as historian Yael Zerubavel has discussed[107]—led to the construction and commemoration of Tel Hai? When Shapira adduces the statement of a Tel Hai worker just *prior* to the attack—"A place once settled is not to be abandoned"[108]—she is not reconstructing the historical course of events, but rather the ideological discourse that made Tel Hai memorable.

Part of the force of the concept of collective memory is that it transforms collective forgetting and other lapses in commonly held notions from simple errors of simple facts into submerged intentions. Thus, Shapira finds part of the answer to her questions by noting, "One of the features distinguishing the Tel Hai myth is the almost total anonymity of the Arab attackers. Their identity was known: They were neighbors of Tel Hai and Kefar Giladi, both before and after the incident. Nonetheless, in the descriptions of the clash, the identity of the attackers was not pointed out; and at a later stage in the development of the myth, they were not alluded to at all."[109] The omission might be made good through careful archival research, were the point to reinforce the core of facts. Shapira is interested rather in knowing what collective memory communicates in what she calls myths. She concludes, therefore, not by publishing the names of the assailants, but by interpreting the virtual text of the omission. The "'canonical' description of the [closely related] attack on Kefar Giladi" indicates that the anonymous attackers were looking for "any French hiding at the place": "this demand added a foreign, nonlocal touch to the Tel Hai episode, as though it did not derive from the sphere of relations between Jews and Arabs in Palestine."[110] In collective memory, if not in historical fact, "The Arabs were marginal to the topic," thus obfuscating "the central Arab claim."[111]

A fuller answer to Shapira's historical question emerges. Why there, why then? The incident took place at a new border between the competing interests of Britain and France after defeat in the First World War put an end to Ottoman hegemony in the Land of Israel. "The decline in security led to the awareness—more a feeling than a rational insight," writes Shapira, "that the Arabs constituted a genuine competitor for Palestine. Not a *potential* competitor (as was the assessment during the Second Aliyah) but, rather, a second full claimant to the right to the land."[112] The myth of Tel Hai is, above all, an ideological defense against that claim.

If Shapira goes beyond the inclusion of memory texts as historical evidence to the analysis of memory as a historical subject in its own right, she remains fully within an older mode of historiography in another respect. She confines her own personal appearance to the preface. Even there, her first-person testimony is telling. "The idea for this book came to me in 1982," she states in the opening line, "after reading an article by Menahem Begin, then prime minister of Israel, entitled 'On Behalf of a War of Choice.' That was at the time of the ill-fated Israeli invasion of Lebanon, and a fierce debate was being waged in Israel between supporters and opponents of the war. While reading Begin's article, it occurred to me that this was the first time in Zionist history that a leading public figure had openly advocated war."[113] The war issued in a time of agonies in Lebanon and also in Israel. A certain Jewish identity, indeed the collective identity of Israel as the Jewish State, was obscured by the terms of debate of the supporters and opponents of the war. Shapira finds a sameness between the "offensive ethos," which she dates to the Arab Rebellion in 1936, and the "defensive ethos" articulated through the incident at Tel Hai. Both appear as choices for war as the analysis suggests in the body of the text, while Shapira herself withdraws from view.

For Howe, the dangers and the memories overtake him, thrusting him back into his own narration at the point where the second-generation Americans cross out of the world of their immigrant elders. The final section (Epilogue apart) of *World of Our Fathers* bears the title "Dispersion," an intentional irony that makes the initial immigrant enclave on the Lower East Side, retrospectively, not a diaspora, but a lost homeland. The first of its two chapters, "Journeys Outward," ends with a section headed, "The New York Intellectuals." Howe's name does not appear in the text. But the notes indicate that Howe is himself the source of a lengthy excerpt at the close of "The New York Intellectuals," as well as the epigraph to the preceding chapter on "The Yiddish Press." He has reached the time of his own memories, and, taken as a whole, the section "The New York Intellectuals" reads as a memoir.

Howe's memory flashes up at a moment of danger. The Jewish radicals of his cohort in the 1930s and 1940s have become established university professors and public intellectuals by the late 1960s, having mostly become neoconservatives along the way. They face the accusations of a younger generation of radicals who rose up to accuse them of betraying the tradition of the Left. Eschewing the distance of a historian's neutrality in favor of a claim to the role of the storyteller drawing on personal experience, Howe responds: "And what the 'leftist' prigs of the sixties failed to understand—or perhaps understood only too well—was that the 'success' with which they kept scaring themselves was simply one of the possibilities of adult life, a possibility, like failure, heavy with moral risks and disappointment." Howe goes on to enumerate those possibilities as the actualities of middle age: "debts, overwork, varicose veins, alimony, drinking, quarrels, hemorrhoids, depletion, the recognition that one might not prove to be another T. S. Eliot, but also some good things, some lessons learned, some 'rags of time' salvaged and precious."[114] It is an old story, perhaps the oldest story of metamorphosis: the shape-changing from youth to age. Youth preaches rupture with the past. Age recognizes identity: the elders remember themselves in the rebelliousness of youth, and recognize as well how much they resemble the elders they had once rebelled against.

The quarrel of the moderns against the ancients, of youth against age, is a common tale, but Howe represents it as a Jewish story. After the war, he recollects, "the world seemed to be opening up, with all its charms, seductions, and falsities. In the thirties the life of the New York writers had been confined: the little magazine as island, the radical sect as cave."[115] The imagery recalls John Donne ("no man is an island . . ."), filtered through Hemingway ("so ask not, for whom the bell tolls") for a critic of American literature, but then suddenly seems to veer toward Qumran, as though *Dissent* and *Commentary* were latter-day Dead Sea Scrolls. As Howe continues, the Jewish contextualization becomes explicit. "Partly they were recapitulating the pattern of immigrant Jewish experience," he writes, "an ingathering of the flock in order to break out into the world."[116] Or in order to re-member himself among the radicals of an earlier era, Howe remembers the past in the social framework of Jewish collective memory. Here and elsewhere, the cohort is called "the New York writers"; but in the paragraph in which the aging memoirist exposes hemorrhoids and depletion, he calls them "the New York *Jewish* intellectuals."[117] And it is in that name that he introduces the closing excerpt from his own previously published work: "Here one Jewish intellectual speaks."[118]

Bahloul is less coy. But then not only does she take her point of departure from the theoretical and methodological postulates of a different discipline, anthropology rather than history, she is also writing after and in full awareness of Yerushalmi's *Zakhor*. She has learned from his misgivings about the capacity of history to function as a metaphorized memory, and she is prepared to press the issue further. "Whereas for Yerushalmi the main question," she argues, "was whether the Jewish commandment of remembrance was supported by a genuine historiographic endeavor, what are now being examined are the symbolic structures and the logic of memorial narrative—how collectivities, more like poets than like historians, elaborate a textual treatment of their past."[119] And citing studies of Ashkenazic, Sephardic, and Mizrahi Jews by members of her own cohort, she adds: "It is no longer the mere social dimension of memory that scholars explore but its narrative logic as well. Thus the most recent approaches to Jewish memory, inspired by hermeneutic anthropology, explore a cultural process based on a concept of time as 'reversible,' that is similar to the construction of mythical narrative."[120]

The conception and internalization of time as a steady, irreversible progression from past to present to future is one of the constitutive elements of human intellection for Kant, and a cornerstone of post-Kantian (i.e., modern) philosophy. For some two centuries, historical reasoning told time in that way: the forward sweep of the clock hands, the mounting numbers of the yearly dates. Einstein's relativity has changed the picture, but Bahloul recalls that mythic time had always been configured otherwise, emphasizing cyclical returns, for instance. Scholar of Kabbalah Elliot Wolfson links the scientific and philosophical bases of a post-Einsteinian conception of time to Jewish mystical thinking when he explicates what he refers to as "timeswerve," or "the reversibility of the temporal flow": "We could, then, think of time's motion as comprising two movements—procession and return—following exactly the same pattern of development in two directions."[121] But the principle is neither mythic nor mystical, if those terms suggest that such reversibility is foreign to the mainstream of Jewish learning. Rather, the talmudic dictum "There is no before or after in Torah" (Pesahim 6b) is fundamental to rabbinic interpretation of Hebrew Scriptures, authorizing, for instance, the regular midrashic practice of citing prooftexts at the greatest remove from a passage under discussion.

Wolfson develops the ground-principle of the timeswerve into a methodology, by representing reversibility through the rhetorical figure of chiasmus, the crossing trope: for example, "Unveiling the Veil/Veiling the Unveiled."[122] He then deploys chiastic formulations on virtually every densely argued page of *Language, Eros, Being* to characterize and elucidate the two-way relationship between concealment and revelation without falling back into the logic of causality and the idiom of the either/or. That is, Wolfson would make kabbalistic thinking—a subset of thinking Jewishly—the mode, no less than the object, of his study.

Bahloul, for her part, both studies and practices reversibility by turning to the *morada*, the dwelling place, rather than to a text, as the site for building memory. More precisely, she reads the house—and not just any house, but specifically Dar-Refayil, the two-story, multi-family dwelling that had been her family's home in Sétif in eastern Algeria—as a canonical text subject to the hermeneutical interventions of her informants expressed as their shared but non-identical memories. "Female and male places, private and collective space, corners for parents and children's nooks, places reserved for hygiene, sexualized places and culinary spaces, places for working and places for resting," she writes, "all these oppositions within domestic space refer to the oppositions structuring social relations."[123] Bahloul organizes this concluding overview as a set of binaries that underwrite her linguistic turn, that is, her reading of architecture as a sign system of social meanings, communicated as "messages and symbols" (in Shapira's words) in the work of re-membering. The repeated "and" of the listing appears to mask the either/or logic of structuralist analysis: a place is male or it is female, a place for work or a place for rest. Yet the collective memory recorded and examined by Bahloul defies simple opposition as the structuring principle of social space: "Memory's reconstruction of Dar-Refayil is riddled with distinctions which it proceeds to transgress."[124]

Of these distinctions, the most fundamental for Jewish Studies is the ethnic boundary that separates off a Jewish "world," thereby circumscribing the field as the space for studying Jews and only Jews. The preeminent locus for the both/and of mixed categories in Dar-Refayil is the central courtyard around which the apartments and the memories of their inhabitants are built: "The starting point for all narratives is the courtyard, which is constructed as representing *togetherness*,"[125] Bahloul writes with emphasis on her alternative paradigm for Jewish Studies as a memory discipline. And by way of illustration, she adds, "It was a collective space, a place for sharing. Jews and Muslims would chat and work there side by side; they would raise their children there together."[126]

Referring to "religious truths" of the Catholic Church, Halbwachs had already recognized that collective memories not only "had to be adjusted to each other," thus providing internal coherence to group identity; they also had to be adjusted "to the ideas and beliefs of all kinds circulating outside."[127] Bahloul's reading of the architecture of memory takes a further step, increasingly characteristic in Jewish Studies, by examining spaces that are neither inside nor outside, or rather are both at once. "In some narratives" of the collective memory of Dar-Refayil, she explains, the courtyard "is an intermediate place between the street and the home, a symbolic extension of each."[128]

Consistent with Kronfeld's strategy of reading the major through the minor, but further along a deconstructive trajectory, Bahloul maps the mixed space of togetherness at the very center of the Jewish dwelling place. Mixture is not limited to a peripheral phenomenon, at a border crossing between the inside of the tradition and the outside of other beliefs and life practices. Rather, the both/and is built into the very midst of lived Jewish environments, Bahloul argues, just as Brettschneider had demonstrated that such togetherness is inscribed in central Jewish texts in her proposal for both a Jewished gender studies and a gendered and queered Jewish Studies.

Archaeologist Cynthia M. Baker maps an intersection in these approaches to the built environment and the textual tradition in her study of talmudic discussions of the *eruv*, a supplementary space constructed to extend the physical and symbolic boundaries of the home with respect to Sabbath restrictions.[129] Baker poses courtyard and alleyway as a theoretical frame through which to reread the intent, if not the method, of rabbinic dicta, arguing for evidence of a circumambient "customary practice," which she finds in a reference in the Mishnah to *dat yehudit*, whose ambiguities she glosses as follows:

> The persistent difficulties posed by this peculiar invocation of courtyard space only add to my sense that this particular appeal to courtyards is likely imported from another discourse altogether—namely, the one about wives covering their heads when 'going out.' These suspicions gain still further impetus from the recognition that it is not simply a peculiar *category of space* that the rabbinic traditions deploy to contain distinctions among women's headgear, but they elsewhere invoke an otherwise unattested *class of law* to address similar 'feminine' concerns: 'Jewish law' or the 'law of the Jewess' (*dat yehudit*).[130]

Baker offers categories of space as a new orienting metaphor for classes of law. Above all, she organizes her approach to the early history of rabbinic law around limit cases, such as the gendered customary practices of "Jewish law/law of the Jewess." On the one hand, the *dat yehudit* concerns itself with courtyards and alleyways and, primarily, the activity of women in them, as the substance of the law. But on the other hand, the courtyard or alleyway is offered as a critical metaphor for the *dat yehudit*. In turning to a talmudic concept for the language in which to articulate a poststructuralist approach to Jewish Studies, Baker takes Jewish learning both as her object of research and also as her tutor.

Such metaphorization is the foundation of Yerushalmi's proposal to contest the hegemonic role of historiography in the formation of Jewish Studies with a disciplinary stance guided by the commandment *zakhor*, remember. He makes the process of metaphorization altogether explicit in his "Postscript" to *Zakhor*:

> For any people there are certain fundamental elements of the past—historical or mythic, often a fusion of both—that become "Torah," be it oral or written, a teaching that is canonical, shared, commanding consensus; and only insofar as this "Torah" becomes "tradition" does it survive. Every group, every people, has its *halakhah*, for *halakhah* is not 'Law,' *nomos*, in the Alexandrian, let alone the Pauline, sense. The Hebrew noun derives from *halakh*, "to walk," hence *halakhah*—the Path on which one walks, the Way, the "Tao"—the complex of rites and beliefs that gives a people its sense of identity and purpose. Only those moments out of the past are transmitted that are felt to be formative or exemplary for the *halakhah* of a people as it is lived in the present; the rest of "history" falls, one might almost say literally, by the "wayside."[131]

Where the sharing of memories and other literary pursuits offer a metaphor for halakhah, and their study contests historiography as a metaphor for Jewish learning in the current state of the question, a metaphorized midrash is also required.

### Understanding Again

Yerushalmi's influential work met a strong challenge from historian Amos Funkenstein. Funkenstein's blunt response—"Yerushalmi exaggerates"[132]—forms part of his broader explication of the "counter-" of "counterhistory." Discussing a series of examples from Christian responses to both Jewish and "pagan" antecedents, to Marx's critique of bourgeois, liberal humanism, to Nazi genocide, Funkenstein depicts changes in the relation of the present to the past as a dialectic of unrelieved conflict. Counterhistory, in this view, is a Hegelian negation, and later a Nazi *Vernichtung* (annihilation), without a Hegelian synthesis that rises above opposition. The charge of exaggeration is really an accusation of reductionism: Yerushalmi's conception of Jewish memory may be nothing more than a counterhistory of Jewish historiography.

Funkenstein notes that the interpretation of the law at the heart of Jewish learning required at least "a modicum of historical awareness" to understand such realia as "the estimated monetary value of coins mentioned in sources [and] the significance of institutions of the past."[133] Moreover, if "normative Judaism did not preserve a continuous record of political events in the form of chronicles or historical studies," as Funkenstein admits, accepting the "basic fact" of Yerushalmi's argument, "it did, however, preserve a continuous and chronological record of legal innovations." Funkenstein adds, "Innovations of halakha were genuine 'historical' happenings, and the term 'innovation' (*chidush*) itself indicates that every halakhic ruling had to have historical, even if fictitious, legitimation."[134] Finally, Funkenstein asserts that the seepage across the conceptual divide also occurs in the opposite direction: professionalized historiography enters the folkish collective memory by way of school books. In sum, historical consciousness, throughout the ages, does not contradict collective memory, but is rather "a developed and organized form of it."[135]

For Yerushalmi and the scholarship oriented by *Zakhor*, memory is the motor of a return to a Jewish mode of understanding identity *in time* (i.e., both temporally and also "before it's too late"). The processes of memory point to Jewish methodologies for studying Jews. For Funkenstein historical consciousness is itself the same return. He charts a foundational moment for "our modern perception of history"—note the participatory possessive—in the sixteenth and seventeenth centuries, when the ancient and medieval "perception of historical facts as self-evident" gave way to the sense that "no historical fact is in and of itself meaningful: only its context endows a historical fact with meaning and significance."[136] But that is only to say that in its turn against the "self-evident," modern history recuperates for all nations "the founding insight of the people of Israel: Jewish culture never took itself for granted."[137] Or, to recall the terms of debate of Wilhelm von Humboldt, modern history was founded as a field not so much for gathering facts, but for discerning their invisible part, that is, interpreting their meaning and significance. And such interpretive labors around the "hermeneutic circle"[138] of contextualization re-member modern Jewish Studies on the rolls of the oldest of Jewish sciences: exegesis. Facts continue to be gathered, of course, but the role of hermeneutics, often as a self-conscious return to both the objects and the modes of Jewish learning, is a chief element in the current state of Jewish Studies.

This hermeneutic turn and return in exemplified in "a significant turning point" in the career of one of the most prolific figures in Jewish Studies: for so Jacob Neusner reflects on his own trajectory as a scholar of the Mishnah.[139] Referring to his prior historiographical work,[140] Neusner notes an impasse: with regard to the delineation of a tradition attached to a named authority, "it seemed to me that such methodological progress as I might make . . . had been attained."[141] Since Neusner's underlying "worldview of 'authorships'" led to a sharp theoretical critique by Daniel Boyarin,[142] it is all the more important to note that in his work on the law of purities, Neusner himself recognized that the focus on authorships "left open the central methodological issue in the study of Talmudic literature for *historical purposes*: How are we to deal with sayings not assigned to an individual authority?"[143]

Previously the identity of the named authority provided the thread of continuity that could be followed forward from that person's own era over a long course of subsequent attributions. But where the sayings are anonymous, it is the substantive point of law that provides the continuity to be traced backward to its earliest recorded instantiation. It is the need to determine the substance of the law that demands the work of exegesis. "The historical purpose of this inquiry must not be obscured by its exegetical form," writes Neusner.[144] His goal, that is, remains to reach an understanding of the law as it was formulated within certain communities of sages at particular moments in time, and thus to provide a historical view of the development of early rabbinic Judaism. Yet the exegetical procedure nonetheless marks a self-conscious return to Jewish learning.

Neusner expresses his awareness of that return in two ways. First, in accordance with academic norms, he begins by situating his work on the mishnaic laws of purities in relation to contemporary scholarship. He will refer repeatedly to that body of work in his discussion, but at the outset his point is to underline the divorce between Jewish Studies and Jewish learning on the part of those who have failed to avail themselves of traditional textual commentary. "Those 'modern' or 'scientific' scholars who have dismissed the achievement of nearly seventeen hundred years of exegetical work, without even examining what they reject," Neusner admonishes, "have not thereby advanced the inquiry but impeded it."[145] Good historical research is not a break with the past of Jewish learning, but rather its extension.

Neusner locates his own exegetical efforts on the layout of the Romm page—that is, the Vilna edition of 1887 that comprehends or, one might say, embraces the text of the Mishnah in commentaries that range up to what were then relatively recent interpretations by late eighteenth- and early nineteenth-century luminaries. "In the great days of the Romm press in Vilna, toward the third quarter of the nineteenth century," Neusner writes, "I might have offered to the editor, Samuel Shraga Feiginsohn, a set of modest glosses, in the hope of finding a small corner on the page for some discrete observations." He adds, "As is clear, once it is no longer possible to take one's place in very small type at the bottom of the Romm page or in some appendix, it is best to find a more sustained mode of presenting ideas."[146] Reading Neusner's previously cited remark chiastically, it is possible to say that one must not allow the modern historiographic form to obscure the exegetical purpose, just as, following Gerson Cohen, one must not allow the historical narrative of Ibn Daud to obscure the homiletic method and intent.

Second, given the exegetical background, Neusner organizes historical knowledge according to a traditional conception of time that contests modern, historicist understandings. Having laid out the forms and formulary patterns and assessed the value of attributions in the third volume of *A History of the Mishnaic Law of Purities*, Neusner takes up the central historical problem of distinguishing between "the traits of the law" in the community of Yavneh and its successor at Usha. To address this question, he says, "our first task is to find appropriate metaphorical language for our inquiry."[147] He then considers the metaphors of "strata" and of "stages," rejecting both for their suggestion of clear separation. Once adopted, such a "metaphor is rapidly reified, so that it becomes natural to discuss the traits of a given stratum wholly apart from those of the next,"[148] whereas the history of the law, like the layout of the Romm page, is characterized by more complex interrelationships of *togetherness*. He turns, or returns, therefore, to the language of the early rabbis for an expression that conveys their own conception of the historical process of the law as a process of exegesis.

To what may a history of mishnaic law be likened? On the one hand, Neusner breaks with a fundamental assumption of traditional Jewish learning, along the bias of scientific, that is, historico-philological scholarship: "I do not take for granted a fundamentally unitary legal corpus . . . and therefore take into account the possibility of repetition, contradiction, and other sorts of imperfections, hitherto regarded as unthinkable."[149] And yet the self-conscious rhetoricity of Neusner's search for the appropriate metaphor to organize knowledge is itself a rabbinic trait and leads to a rabbinic solution: *massekhet*, referring literally to "a web on a loom" in Neusner's gloss,[150] which is the term used to designate a tractate of the Mishnah. "So in using the metaphor of *massekhet* the Amoraim [the generation of rabbinic sages following the Pharisees and then the Tannaim] seem to have meant, 'a web of coherent law, part of a far larger fabric of law, itself composed of numerous individual strands of thread.'"[151] By recourse to the same metaphor of weaving (e.g., his chapter titles, "The Weaving of the Law: Yavneh and Usha," "The Weavers of the Law"), Neusner implicitly organizes history in tractates. His exegetical history is not simply a continuation of the mishnaic fabric, but a metaphorization of the mishnaic procedure.

As from Mishnah and Talmud, so from Midrash, the rabbinic tradition of biblical interpretation, which continues to be an oral practice in contemporary homilies at the synagogue and in other extra-mural venues of Jewish adult education as well as a written form in academic scholarship and publications for a more general readership. Among the midrashic techniques metaphorized for Jewish Studies, the process of "reading in" is of special note in the current state of the field.

Nothing less than a determined effort to accomplish this work has been needed to redress gender imbalance. Feminist contributions to the current state of Jewish Studies, and most particularly to the study of rabbinic literature, constitute a wholesale exercise of reading in, exemplified in the pioneering work of feminist theorist and theologian Judith Plaskow. "Modern historiography," Plaskow writes, "assumes precisely that the original 'revelation,' at least as we have it, is not sufficient, that there are enormous gaps both in tradition and in the scriptural record, that to recapture women's experiences we need to go behind our records and *add* to them, acknowledging that that is what we are doing."[152] Plaskow's proposal, anything but modest, carries Jewish Studies both back and forth along a timeswerve: back to the stance of traditional Jewish learning and forth around the "posts-" of contemporary theoretical discourse.

To follow Plaskow back to traditional midrashic procedures and forward beyond theories of identity and its politics, it is necessary to examine the particular character of her addition. As a polemical, or even revolutionary stance, Plaskow's feminist adding does not mean more of the same, more of the sameness. Studying courtyards as the space of the *dat yehudit* is not like raising the dormer or building an extension to the kitchen, that is, more house. Rather, Baker's account of courtyards traces a supplement to domestic space in the early rabbinic period in two senses: *both* an added, adjacent work area, *and also* a deconstructive wedge that overburdens the received dichotomies of prescriptive statements, such as the laws of purity dividing clean from unclean.

In a similar vein, and for similar feminist purposes, one finds Chava Weissler taking up the "courtyard texts," as it were, of Yiddish devotional literature of the early modern period with a large female readership. From the position of these supplements to canonical Hebrew sources, she is able to examine the mixed categories of "men who are like women" and "women who are like men" that are absent from halakhic construction of gender.[153] So, too, Elisheva Baumgarten turns from the substance of the law to family history, where she finds in the metaphorical alleyways of medieval Ashkenaz "the shared facets of Jewish and Christian practice and belief,"[154] against the grain of both Jewish learning and Jewish Studies, at least in the Ashkenazic domain. It is primarily through feminist studies that theories of alterity have come to supplement theories of identity in Jewish Studies. All that had been read out—the wide spectrum of gender and sexuality, so-called "peripheral" geographies, practices at odds with "normative" Judaism, and "other differences," to recall the title of Jonathan and Daniel Boyarin's pivotal collection of essays—has begun to be read in, making Jewish Studies more hospitable.

A more recent collection, and a showcase of the new hospitality, *Cultures of the Jews*, edited by historian David Biale, demonstrates the impact of otherness: the provincializing of Jewish Studies.[155] Islamicist Lucette Valensi speaks in a representative voice in her contribution to Biale's volume, when she observes: "Trained in the general, classical tradition, North African Jewish scholars developed a specific variety [of written tradition], with its own set of references—other local scholars—and its own particular audience." She continues: "Convinced of the centrality of their own community, they rarely tried to measure themselves against other centers of the Diaspora. In the process, a kind of introversion of the common culture occurred, together with the embeddedness within local settings."[156] That embeddedness made cultural negotiation as much a constant of North African Jewish life as was commercial transaction. Thus, in a separate volume on a related cultural context, and under the heading of an epigraph from Biale—"The issue is not influence, but interaction"—literary scholar Marc S. Bernstein investigates the movement of variants of the popular tale of "Our Master Joseph the Righteous" as a case study of "the transfer of cultural artifacts between Judaism and Islam."[157]

These fluid and interactive social processes have led to a transformation of the concept of ethnic boundaries to a mapping of permeable *borders* across the vast geography of Jewish Studies. A new key word is emerging, along with a range of cognates.[158] Jewish Studies, and not only Jewish Studies, increasingly finds Jews, as allied fields find their subjects, dwelling in the metaphorical courtyard. As a result, there are now many new theoretical models available, largely generated in allied fields, to articulate cultural contact in the border zones, in which all parties are both imitating and imitated, in a complex balance of mimesis and alterity.[159]

The border is always in the middle of somewhere and, often enough, in the middle of "the" Jews. (Biale rewrites "the culture" as the plural "cultures" in his title, but it will require a new key in Jewish Studies to learn to eliminate the "the" that so frequently universalizes some Jews as "the Jews," or worse yet, "the Jew.") Valensi draws and crosses that border as the other differences negotiated between immigrant Jews from Italy, especially Livorno, and the native Twansa Jews of Tunisia. And even the center cannot hold: Paula E. Hyman has long since provincialized Ashkenaz by reading Alsace as the site of the "development of modern communal institutions and new forms of Jewish culture,"[160] and not merely a byway on the route to a modernity located on the straight and narrow path from Berlin to Paris. Furthermore, Hyman recognizes the life practices of Jewish masses as no less central than the ideologies and acculturations of the religious, intellectual, and economic elites.

In her discussion of the turn-of-twentieth-century Ottoman Empire, Sarah Abrevaya Stein extends this approach to an overdetermined supplementary space: Sephardic, but neither Iberian nor Golden Age; Jewish language, but neither Yiddish nor Hebrew; and advertisements in a newspaper, not journalism, much less "literature." She presents a hatless man in Western-style clothing sitting at the dinner table, chin in hand, contemplating a dish that he is plainly hesitant to eat, in an advertisement that appeared in the Ladino newspaper *El tiempo*, in Istanbul in August 1910. It is the very picture of uncertainty and discomfort. Here the border runs through the man himself, dividing his sartorial from his gastronomic tastes: on the one side, his willingness to don the appropriate fashion of new customs, like "the act of eating outside the home"; on the other, his unwillingness to partake of the meal.[161] You can lead this Ottoman Jew to table, but you can't make him eat. The caption frames the issue as a matter of physiology, rather than conflicted desire, and offers a remedy in the form of "Pink Pills." But it may be that the Hebrew letters of the Ladino text are themselves as much a part of the problem as they are the cure. For they both serve to usher their reading public into the institutions and discourses of modernity—the periodical press, mass-media advertisement, the medicalization of culture—and to mark their alienation from the national milieu in which they are embedded, as Jews speaking a separate Jewish language. Stein comments, "In truth, the indigestion to which Pink Pills' advertisements referred was not so much corporeal as symbolic. Even if Sephardi diets were slow to change, anxieties about digestion and appetite were being born of a hyper-consciousness about food consumption and health that was stoked by the press itself."[162] But the apparent health issue is a metaphorization of *kashrut*, Jewish dietary laws, which constitute a far older hyper-consciousness about food consumption.

Literary critic and Yiddishist Ruth Wisse remarks on much the same phenomenon in the case of Franz Kafka, perhaps the only author of Jewish fiction not writing in a "Jewish language" whose place in what Wisse calls "the modern Jewish canon," appears, after nearly a century, unimpeachably secure.[163] Wisse asserts that Kafka "had been born into the German language and to this body he felt himself condemned irrespective of how much he exercised it and what repertoire he performed."[164] Alluding to the tuberculosis that killed him and perhaps to his peculiarities at table that now might be diagnosed as an eating disorder, Wisse continues: "Kafka's adversarial relation to his body is the organic source of his adversarial relation to his language—or perhaps it is the other way around, with the poisoned language affecting the body's health."[165] Wisse's response aims to promote the health of Jewish Studies. Against internal division, she would reaffirm the boundaries of ethnic identity, constructing a canon on the principle of mutual recognition: "In Jewish literature the authors or characters know and let the reader know that they are Jews."[166]

Yet reading from the minor to the major, from a Ladino ad for Pink Pills to the writing of Franz Kafka, it appears that Ladino is neither more nor less poisonous than a "non-Jewish language." Jews live on both sides of many borders—Judeo-Arabic and Italian in the case of nineteenth-century Tunisian Jews; German and Yiddish and Czech in Kafka's Prague: Ladino and Turkish and Greek and Arabic and Serbian and on and on in the Ottoman Empire; but also the borders between any of these vernaculars, whether considered "Jewish language" or not, and Hebrew as holy tongue, with further borderlines between Hebrew and Aramaic dating back to the Bible itself (Gen. 31:47).

Like many peoples, Jews have generally lived within what linguist and literary critic Benjamin Harshav refers to as the linguistic polysystem.[167] The crucial issue in Stein's reading of the Ladino ad and Wisse's reflection on Kafka is the construction of Jewish lives along linguistic and other cultural borders as a source of corporeal and symbolic complaint, an adversarial relationship, a house divided that cannot stand. The sense of threat is registered in the public sphere in current efforts at studying Jews demographically, and the often acrimonious debate in which the findings are discussed in periodical publications. The social scientific evidence points to decreasing numbers of Jews affiliated with congregations, of Jews born in Israel and remaining in Israel, of Jews married to other Jews, in short, to the number of Jews at all. Not infrequently, the news is heralded as a threat to survival and, at its most extreme, as a posthumous victory for Hitler.

The social responses are generally oriented by theories of identity. Jewish education—from post–bar and bat mitzvah programs for very young adults, to Project Birthright trips to Israel for twenty-somethings, to lecture series for their parents and for seniors—is most often conceived as remedial reconstruction of commonalities. In this view, somewhere within those shifting peripheries there is a core of sameness. Hence, Wisse says in *The Modern Jewish Canon*, "I would not expect anyone's list to exclude the books I have chosen, they are free to make a case for additional writers."[168] Jewish education is generally charged with transmitting the contents of such a core curriculum. Moreover, the very act of participating in Jewish education programs is expected to provide shared experiences on the basis of those Jewish contents. Shared experiences will mean collective memories; shared knowledge will mean mutual recognition. Even if Jewish Studies programs in non-sectarian university settings cannot avow to this Jewish community building as a mission, they may serve these purposes as well.

But it is also possible to reconceive Jewish Studies on the basis of theories of alterity, heterogeneity, provinciality. Canons begin with exclusions, after all, as Wisse readily admits. In her case, for instance, the "the modern Jewish canon" is explicitly a modern Ashkenazic core curriculum: "I have limited myself to works of Ashkenazi Jews and their descendents," she writes.[169] In contrast, literary critic Susan Gubar pursues a decidedly anti-canonical strategy in *Poetry after Auschwitz*:

> As I discovered poet after poet struggling to keep cultural memory of the Holocaust alive, I became upset with the currently available anthologies, critical works, and courses on the Shoah, all of which appeared uninflected by the verse on which I was stumbling. If no one knows about these texts, I worried, would they simply slip into oblivion? Of course, I had another option: putting together a collection of verse. Although such a volume should eventually come into being, it seems too soon to canonize a tradition very much in the making. Instead, I decided to chance speculations that are meant to be provisional, not definitive, an impetus for further study by others.[170]

Like a canon, an anthology circumscribes the grounds of commonality and so becomes a vehicle of collective memory and, for Jewish anthologies, a delineation of ethnic identity. But canons and anthologies and all closed collections are also, chiastically, forms of foreclosure. As Gubar's alternative commitment to heterogeneity recalls, an anthology aids recollection of the material selected, while at the same time it invites the forgetting of other voices—voices speaking for otherness. Her anxiety that the texts of Holocaust poetry might be forgotten echoes the prior and more profound anxiety, incited by the taunts of the perpetrators, that the Shoah itself might slip into oblivion. The loss of a single poem, a single voice, is inestimable; to save a voice from oblivion is perhaps to save a world.

# 3    In a New Key

## Cast of Characters

*André Aciman*, contemporary memoirist, essayist, literary critic who emigrated in his youth with most of the Egyptian Jewish community.

*Martin Buber*, Jewish philosopher, disseminator of Hassidic lore, and an early, idiosyncratic Zionist; born in Galicia, resettled in Germany, and made aliyah, where he was among the first generation of faculty members of the Hebrew University.

*Franz Rosenzweig*, German-born Jewish philosopher, known to a restricted circle in his lifetime, eventually recognized as a key voice in Jewish thought of the twentieth century; translator of *Jehuda Halevy* and, in collaboration with *Buber*, of the Hebrew Scriptures; he has been onstage, if often unseen, from the opening lines of the Introduction.

*Yosef Hayim Yerushalmi*, contemporary Jewish historian and theorist of Jewish memory, who had a leading role in chapter 2.

*Edmond Jabès*, Egyptian Jewish French-language novelist and poet.

*Benjamin Zucker*, Jewish gem merchant and contemporary novelist, devoted to *Franz Kafka*, Bob Dylan, and James Joyce.

*Elliot Wolfson*, contemporary Jewish scholar of the Kabbalah; his conceptualization of the timeswerve figured in chapter 2 and returns as a key to chapter 3.

*S. Y. Agnon*, Galician-born Jewish storyteller and novelist, a founding figure of Israeli fiction.

*Jehuda Halevi*, Jewish poet and philosopher of medieval Iberia, who died en route to Zion.

*Jonathan Safran Foer*, contemporary American Jewish novelist; husband of *Nicole Krauss*.

*Robert Frost*, twentieth-century American poet, whose verse appeared in Mr. Engel's sixth-grade lesson in the old Ardsley Middle School.

*Emmanuel Lévinas*, Jewish philosopher and also teacher of Talmud outside the study house; born in Lithuania, studied in France, then Germany, finally returning to France; stands in relation to Jewish thought in a new key as *Rosenzweig* does to the current state of the question.

*Kadya Molodowsky*, Jewish poet writing in Yiddish, born in Belarus, immigrated to the United States before the outbreak of the Second World War, and thereafter lived in both the newly founded State of Israel and the United States.

*R. B.* [Ronald Brooks] *Kitaj*, American-born Jewish painter, and author of two *diasporist* manifestos, long active in England, but returned to the United States in the wake of a controversy concerning his penchant for appending midrashic commentaries to his own paintings.

*Walter Benjamin*, a Jew who fled Nazi Germany and then tried to flee farther from France, failed, and committed suicide at the Spanish border; philosopher, literary critic, cultural theorist; lifelong friend and correspondent of *Gershom Scholem*; a constant companion in my Jewish Studies classes.

*Cynthia Ozick*, contemporary American Jewish fiction writer and sometime essayist.

*Michael Fishbane*, contemporary American Jewish scholar of Bible and Midrash.

*Harold Bloom*, contemporary American Jewish scholar of literature and literary theory, and my teacher.

*Gershom Scholem*, Israeli Jewish scholar of Jewish mysticism, born in Germany; probably the most widely respected figure in Jewish Studies in the later twentieth century; lifelong friend and editor of *Benjamin*.

*Erich Reiss*, him, I don't know, as Robert De Niro tells Billy Crystal in *Analyze This*.

*Theodor Adorno*, Jewish philosopher born in Germany, exiled in the United States during the Nazi years, returned to East Germany after the war.

*Gillian Rose*, British Jewish philosopher, who made a deathbed conversion to Christianity.

*Joseph Green*, Polish-born Jew who made his career as a director of Yiddish-language films in the United States.

*Severo Sarduy*, in the summer of 1983, at a café in Paris just around the corner from the offices of the French publishing house Editions du Seuil, where he worked, and on the strength of an introduction by my teacher, Roberto González Echevarría, Sarduy told me a story: Gabriel García Márquez had been passing through Cuba not long before and stopped at the home of Sarduy's parents to express to them his great esteem for their son's novels and to ask, for that reason, if there were not something that he, García Márquez, might do for them, given the privileges of his position in the world of literature and in Cuba, owing to his unwavering support of the Revolution. He asked if he could buy them a new refrigerator, for instance. "But what would Jewish parents say?" Sarduy asked rhetorically. "We want to see our son. We'll come back to Cuba. We promise. We just want to see our son. Can you arrange visas?" And so García Márquez did. "They're arriving tomorrow," Sarduy added, thereby explaining his need to hasten away. He picked up the check, but the foreshortening of the conversation meant that further discussion of a job opportunity that he mentioned would have to wait, and I could not. I trust he had a joyful reunion, while I returned to the United States, to the relief of my Jewish parents, completed a dissertation in comparative literature, and mourned Sarduy's early death.

*Franz Kafka*, favorite Jewish artist of *Kitaj*; mine, too.

*Bathsheba, Hélène Cixous*, and *Rembrandt von Rijn*, the last, the seventeenth-century Dutch painter, studied Jews by painting them, among other subjects; the first was among the Jews thus studied; both are studied in turn by Cixous, a Jew from Algeria, contemporary French-language author of fiction, drama, essays, memoirs, and also a philosopher and feminist theorist.

*Jonathan Boyarin*, contemporary Jewish anthropologist and theorist of Jewish Studies; we have met him before, often in the company of his brother Daniel.

*Shulamith Hareven*, born in Warsaw, contemporary Israeli-Jewish novelist, essayist and story writer.

*Jacques Derrida*, another Jew from Algeria and friend of *Cixous*; a philosopher; another teacher of mine.

*Robert Alter*, contemporary Jewish scholar of modern Jewish literature; English-language translator of and commentator on Hebrew Scriptures.

*Bruno Schulz*, Polish-language Jewish fiction writer from the interwar period; murdered by the Nazis in his home town in Poland.

*Moshe Idel*, Romanian-born contemporary Israeli Jewish scholar of kabbalah.

*Nicole Krauss*, contemporary American Jewish novelist, wife of *Jonathan Safran Foer*.

*Leslie Brisman*, American Jewish literary critic and scholar of Midrash; teacher of one of the first Fishman Faculty Seminars in Jewish Studies at Vassar College.

*Martin Ritt*, contemporary American Jewish film director, blacklisted during the McCarthy period; his *Norma Rae* was the subject of conversation in class yesterday; those who took part—*Nathan, Will, Ria, Jenn, Lara, Rachel, Bianca, Marni, Fiona, Sara*, and *Evan* may stand for the many, many students who are also always present in these pages.

*Susan Sontag*, American Jewish novelist and cultural critic.

*Philip Levine*, contemporary American-Jewish poet.

*The setting is an open house in Berlin, circa 1800 or, alternatively, a Jewish Studies classroom in the leisurely, animated atmosphere before the teacher arrives. Many conversations are taking place at once; overhearing, the ear picks*

*out now one fragment, now another. As conversation moves, the cast of charac-
ters, who are all present on stage at all times, appear to form different groupings,
which may fade from view, dissolve, take new shapes. They constitute what
Benjamin calls constellations. There are countless other stars visible from other,
equally contingent points of view, and countless other possible configurations.
It may nevertheless be true that there is but one firmament.*

## Points of Departure

*On the final pages of his memoir, André Aciman recalls* the eve of his departure
from his native city of Alexandria, a moment following the Passover meal
commemorating the biblical Exodus. "Exactly a year from now, I vowed,
I would sit outside at night wherever I was," he writes, "somewhere in
Europe, or in America, and turn my face to Egypt, as Moslems do when
they pray and face Mecca, and remember this night, and how I had
thought these things and made this vow."[1] Embedded still in his heterogeneous locale, confident of its centrality, Aciman builds a new Passover
ritual with Egyptian bricks and mortar upon the foundations of the closing exhortation of the Haggadah: "Next year in Jerusalem." The hybridity
is nothing new; but the newness is something strange. The strange
temporality of the new, this proleptic remembrance of things not yet past:
how would one say which of the words that we use now will have
emerged as the keys of a conversation still to come? With all the vows that
we annul, which will be the promises to keep? Which the thoughts that
we retain? Which facing, and whither, will become the stance of prayer?

*The as yet little-known Franz Rosenzweig responds* in a letter to the republication of a set of lectures by Martin Buber, a leading figure in the Jewish
Studies that he called the Hebrew Renaissance. It is a second thought.
Rosenzweig had read the lectures years before, when they were obscured
"in the heat of battle into which your thoughts dragged us," he recalls.
A new edition calls for a new reading: "now that we re-read them with
calm," he writes, "and yet not too objectively but with, so to say, autobiographical excitement, we see clearly that it was our own words to which
you were the first to give expression."[2] How will we find our own words
in the words of our teachers? How will we teach so that our students
hear our words and overhear their own? And how, in transmitting and
receiving a teaching, will teacher and student alike recognize what is key
in what is new?

Rosenzweig finds a model for his new reading at the outset of one
of the lectures, where Buber had begun by commenting on an epigraph,
a talmudic dictum: "'God's writing engraved on the tablets'—read
not *harut* (engraved) but *herut* (freedom)."[3] The teaching draws on the

ambiguities of the unpointed Hebrew of the biblical text; it practices the freedom, altogether traditional in rabbinic exegesis, that it preaches. Rosenzweig begins his letter by taking just that liberty. He re-cites: "And all thy children shall be taught of the Lord, and great shall be the peace of thy Children! (Isaiah 54:13). Do not read 'banayikh,' thy children, but 'bonayikh,' thy builders."[4] The otherwise unconnected talmudic dicta and their disparate biblical references become call and response. Your "freedom," your preferential reading of freedom over the engraved letter of the law, is my building, my understanding of filiation as edification, a raising up, a transcendence. Read not youth, but builders.

*Y. H. Yerushalmi was in France at the time* of a Holocaust perpetrator trial, delivering a lecture at a conference organized on the topic "The Uses of Forgetting." He noted there, "The Holocaust has already engendered more historical research than any single event in Jewish history, but I have no doubt whatever that its image is being shaped, not at the historian's anvil, but in the novelist's crucible."[5] In the novelist's crucible, yes, and in the poet's profession. Novels and poems: "variable space of hospitality,"[6] a tent, open on four sides, loosely pegged, places of welcome to new voices, a shelter to new conceptualizations, told as images—and not only the image of the Shoah, but of Jewish Studies in a new key, too.

A new Jewish Studies may be a postscript. Poststructuralist, postmodern, postcolonial, postrabbinic: the post is our time signature. But the post- is not only a sign of the time, not simply equivalent to "later than." The post- is posthistorical. The post- reads history as the boundaries of what may be known, at any given conjuncture, from beyond those boundaries. The post- is an outpost. A new Jewish Studies is a fiction. A novel, for instance, as Benjamin Zucker identifies *Blue* and its sequel, or postscript, *Green*, on their respective title pages, despite the unfamiliar configuration of their layout.

A continuous narrative occupies the center of each odd-numbered page in Zucker's two volumes. That "central text," as Zucker explains in his prefatory "Guide to the Reader," is surrounded by marginal commentaries delivered in the name of historical personages and fictional characters, the latter generally forebears of the main protagonists of the "central text."[7] The typographical antecedent is made explicit: "'My grandfather is staring at that page of Talmud, printed in Vilna some twenty years before. The Talmud was given to him by his father-in-law. The manuscript pages surrounding the text were annotations written by his father-in-law and manuscripts from his father-in-law's library. My grandfather, Gutman Gutwirth, was dreaming of traveling to Antwerp,'" reads a portion of the central text in *Green*.[8]

Which the text? The pretext? The postscript? "The pictures offer further commentary on the text," Zucker states in his Guide. "And yet the central text and the commentary itself may also be seen as commentary on the pictures." More generally, Zucker proposes that it is possible to "read this novel forward or backward, circularly or in a linear vector," which is to say, in Elliot Wolfson's idiom, that it is constructed along the timeswerve.[9]

A commentary to the words "Gutman [Gutwirth] was dreaming of voyaging to Antwerp," from that central text in *Green*, appear, in the right margin, where it is ascribed to the father-in-law of protagonist Fisher's grandfather. The commentator further explicates the complex temporality of the gift of the Talmud. "What was I to say to Gutman?" the father-in-law Abish Rheingold asks on the virtual eve of departure. "He had my treasure, my daughter Chaya." "But if she leaves, she takes her father's treasure, too. [Gutman] was also my treasure, my greatest student. Did I not rise before him when he entered my room?"[10] A student is not a hired laborer, and Abish Rheingold is not Laban; he does not oppose the departure, even on second thought. "For I knew that while I was his Rabbi, in the world to come, he would be the commentary on my work."[11] Jewish Studies renews itself as commentary and renews commentary as study.

Zucker offers an image: "I've already given you the key. Simply write the history" is the advice given to Fisher by Abraham Tal, who had been the central figure of the central text of *Blue*.[12] At the upper right margin a commentary by the grandmother of Fisher's lover, Dosha, sets family history in the context of the Shoah. At the upper left, Dosha's grandfather comments on the subsequent line from the same passage in the central text: "'Of course Tal wants you to have his key, darling,' Dosha had told Fisher." The grandfather, however, recalls his Jewish learning: "We learn from the Heilige (holy) Rashi. It is not only the words that matter, it is the line endings that matter. And it is not only the words that matter and the line endings but the spaces between the words and the lines, according to the Zohar Hakodesh, the Holy Zohar. . . . Read not, Rashi would say, his key, darling 'Dosha' but read: 'his key: Darling Dosha.' For Dosha is Tal's key to the world above."[13] Building the new on the freedom of the old. She is his key; read, she is his student.

"'A key,' Fisher mused on Tal's phrase" within the central text of *Green*, which, therefore, already includes commentary on itself: "A word that Tal used with disquieting frequency."[14]

---

*"I stood before the locked door, the key of which I had lost,"* reflected a guest for the night in the fictional town of Szibuch, whose model was the Galician

town of Buczacz, as the model for the guest was the author himself, S. Y. Agnon.[15] The locked door was the entrance to the study house of Szibuch, which no one attended any longer after the war, the Great War, the civil war of Whites and Reds, the pogroms. The guest had been given the key—as hospitality instructs—the sign and means of untrammeled access to tradition. And he, in turn, had begun to dedicate himself to reopening the site of Jewish learning. But now the key was missing.

"Daniel Bach found me standing perplexed. 'Where are your feet bound to?' said he. 'To look for the locksmith,' said I." Because there were towns, perhaps there still are, where the loss of the key to the house of study is no loss, because there is a locksmith who can make good the loss, because the community at large is such a locksmith, whose way cannot be barred, because one knows the contents of Jewish learning even without reopening the door. "Daniel slapped his wooden leg and said, 'Now on your way, my dear, and help us go.'"[16] Because your feet know where they're bound, especially here, in your home town, even after many years, and because a wooden leg, like a substitute key, will still get you there.

"'This is the gentleman who wishes to have a key made,' said Bach to the locksmith." Was an introduction, a re-introduction, necessary? "The locksmith greeted me, clasping my hand joyfully, and I too rejoiced." For whom should he ply his trade, if not for one who seeks reentry? "First, because he would make me the key, and second, because when I was a child I used to stand at the entrance to his shop, looking at the keys and locks." Back then, a child before the locksmith's door, the guest "longed for a chest with a key and a lock. When, later, I gave up the idea of the chest I did not give up the idea of the key."[17] And now, too, he retains the idea of the key, even if not the key itself.

Agnon completes the idea of the key as a Zionist allegory. The guest eventually returns to his new home in the Land of Israel, and unpacking there, he finds among his things, the lost key. The original key to the house of study is (only) to be rediscovered in the Land.

The boy who would become that man, however, had a different idea of the key: "I would lie in bed at night thinking of it—a large, heavy key, the kind a man takes out of his pocket to open his house."[18] Unless it is the same door and the same key, unless any house that opens to the turn of a key—lost, recovered, yours—is a house of study. "I pictured this key in various shapes, but all the shapes were less important than its function and final purpose: the act of opening. Imagine it: In the center of the city stands a house and that house has a door, like all the other houses, and on the door hangs a lock. Along comes a child from school, puts his hand in his pocket, takes out a key, pushes the key into the lock, and twists it this way and that—and immediately the whole house is open before him. What is there in that house?"[19]

*It was said in Sepharad* by Jehuda Halevi, yearning for Zion, "My heart is in the east, and I on the westernmost edge." Rosenzweig, his translator, finds here "a turning point in the history of Jewish exile." He comments: "For a millennium, after the heroic convulsions of the first centuries had ebbed in the study halls of Babylon"—so even Jewish learning may be a falling away—"the longing for Zion remains a dead commodity—religion. . . . Jehuda Halevi's lonely spiritual destiny," that is his commitment to Zion as the site of a necessary return, "is the first beacon of the new movement which then carries on to our present."[20]

It is said by the Sephardim in the generations following expulsion from Spain, and to this day, "we left with the keys to our houses in our hands." The houses are gone, the keys remain. There are many turning points. Turn it and turn it: the heart may also tend toward the westernmost edge.

*Another guest for another night, returning, eastward*, to another hometown after another war, after Auschwitz. Only in Jonathan Safran Foer's tale, the passing of generations means that the guest returns to a town that was never his own home, in search of memories that, likewise, were never quite his own. *Everything Is Illuminated*, Foer's first novel, wins the National Jewish Book Award in the United States.[21]

It is time for a second novel. The niche is there. Another Jewish Book, another award? Foer imagines a child, the son of a man who died in the attack on the Twin Towers, and grandson of German survivors of the Dresden bombing. The book is devoid, one might say, of "Jewish content." Unless not everything is illuminated. Unless there is also an unspoken Jewish aspect, an unsuspected key to every page.

In Foer's new quest the child is a searcher who has a key, but cannot find the lock. Is there a locksmith, a community of locksmiths, to find or forge a lock to fit a key?

And then suddenly, on the page facing the photo of a key on a cord, the child reports that the search is over. "'Where were you? I was worried,'" his grandfather wants to know. "I told him, 'I found the lock.'"

> "You found it?" I nodded. "And?"
>
>   I didn't know what to say. I found it and now I can stop looking? I found it and it had nothing to do with Dad? I found it and now I'll wear heavy boots for the rest of my life?

"I wish I hadn't found it." "It wasn't what you were looking for?" "That's not it." "Then what?" "I found it and now I can't look for it." I could tell he didn't understand me. "Looking for it let me stay close to him for a little while longer." "But won't you always be close to him?" I knew the truth. "No."[22]

---

*The Baal Shem Tov would withdraw to the woods, it is said*, to stand under a particular tree, chant a particular melody, a *niggun*, with particular words, and God granted his petition. In the next generation, his son knew the tree and the melody, but not the words. And it was enough. And the petition was granted. And the grandson knew the tree, but not the melody, and the petition was granted. And what shall we do, in our day, when we know not the tree?

"Two roads diverged in a yellow wood":[23] it was my first lesson in poetry. And yet, not always knowing how way leads on to way, turn and turn about, diverging paths converge again on the return route. We may have only seemed to miss our tree, our door; our approach a path less traveled by; our silence our petition.

---

*Walter Benjamin attempted several times to write* a memoir of his childhood in a bourgeois Berlin Jewish milieu. None of these texts was published in his lifetime. The final version begins with a brief explanation of the origins of the project: "In 1932, when I was abroad, it began to be clear to me that I would soon have to bid a long, perhaps lasting farewell to the city of my birth."[24] Imagining himself on the far side of that breach, looking forward to the moment when travel abroad would turn definitively into exile, and then looking back from there, Benjamin adopts a medical discourse, rather than a metaphorization of prayer. "Several times in my inner life, I had already experienced the process of inoculation as something salutary," he explained. "In this situation, too, I resolved to follow suit, and I deliberately called to mind those images which, in exile, are most apt to waken homesickness: images of childhood." He then offers a theoretical coda concerning the efficacy of the homeopathic cure: "I sought to limit its effect [i.e., of the venom of homesickness] through insight into the irretrievability—not the contingent biographical but the necessary social irretrievability—of the past."[25] It is a modern perspective: geographical displacement, whether voluntary or coerced, is a metaphor for expulsion from a past radically discontinuous with the present. Even were biographical contingences removed—were he not a German Jew in the 1930s—the past was a dead end.

To prolong the existence of the past in the inner life would be to succumb to melancholia. In Benjamin's own terms, that extension is the way of translation. The true translator comes not in the life of the work of art, but after its death; the translation is a survival in the sense of an afterlife. Benjamin does not reminisce about his childhood so much as he translates it.

Benjamin himself recalls the kabbalistic "fragments of a vessel" in explicating the task of the tranlsator.[26] The original and translation do not resemble one another. Rather, they fit together as two fragments (the original no less fragmentary than the translation) along the irregular line of that primordial break between languages. The jagged line of translation is an alternative to the straightforward logic of the essay, for instance; the broken edge is the mark of irretrievability.

"Sexual Awakening," the final fragment in Benjamin's translation of his childhood, is lifted from the earlier "Berlin Chronicle" and placed alongside the fragment "Carousel," in a space outside the table of contents of the final "Berlin Childhood": a non-contents, uncontained, uncontainable. An abridged account from the 1932 version:

> Many years earlier, in one of the streets I passed along on my endless wanderings, I was surprised by the first stirring of my sexual urge, under the oddest circumstances. It was on the Jewish New Year's Day, and my parents had made arrangements for me to attend some religious celebration. . . . I had been entrusted to a relative, whom I had to fetch on my way. But whether because I had forgotten his address or because I was unfamiliar with the district, it grew later and later without my drawing nearer to my goal. . . . While I was wandering thus, I was suddenly and simultaneously overcome, on the one hand, by the thought, "Too late, time was up long ago, you'll never get there"—and, on the other, by a sense of the insignificance of all this. . . . And these two streams of consciousness converged irresistibly in an immense pleasure that filled me with blasphemous indifference toward the service, but exalted the street in which I stood, as if it had already intimated to me the services of procurement it was later to render to my awakened drive.[27]

Despite the title, the incident does not describe a precocious erotic encounter, but rather offers a fragmentary original (a moment mixing release from the norms of his social world, blasphemy, and pleasurable physical sensation) for which Benjamin's later procurement of prostitutes in the quarter of the same synagogue is a translation. The synagogue service is not likened to prostitution, but rather stands behind or beyond both original and translation: a figure of the irretrievable.

⸻

*Aciman opens the first essay of his second book as a postscript* to his personal exodus: "To those who asked, I said I went back to touch and breathe the past again, to walk in shoes I hadn't worn in years. This, after all, was what everyone said when they returned from Alexandria."[28] Returned *from* after returning *to*, that is, either way, any way, all ways, a return: *teshuvah*, both return and also repentance. Emmanuel Lévinas remarks, "What characterizes contemporary Jewish thought after Rosenzweig is that special new experience of the Return. It touches even those formed by tradition, but who rethink that tradition as if returning from some remote West, needing to learn everything."[29] Or some remote East, like Alexandria. Against the ruptures of all modernities recorded as history, the canceled dream of continuity survives in the trope of return across the breach.

Charted as a participation in, recuperation of or remembering an earlier state of things, Return is usually understood to mean the arrival at and of the same. What, then, would be different, what would be new in the "special *new* experience of the Return"? And what key, a century after Rosenzweig, would make the experience of the Return new in Jewish Studies? Lévinas is Rosenzweig's treasure and so he is Rosenzweig's commentary in a new key, author of new meta-tropes for Jewish Studies. Above all, Rosenzweig's Return becomes a *turning toward* the Face of the Other in Lévinas, a *facing*.

Facing Alexandria, for instance, is not yet prayer, but the attitude of prayer, not the Return (like the pilgrimage to Mecca), but already the turning toward. Such facing is the *saying* (le Dire) of prayer in Lévinas's terms, rather than the prayer *said* (le Dit): "[Saying] is the proximity of one to the other, the commitment of an approach, the one for the other, the very signifyingness of signification. (But is approach to be defined by commitment and not rather commitment by approach? . . . ) The original or pre-original saying . . . weaves an intrigue of responsibility."[30] The saying, the prayer of saying: "bring forth my saying" (mayn zog), prays Kadya Molodowsky, "[my] escaping from my being."[31]

This Other is not another Me, more of the same, more ontology, but rather, for all of the Other's proximity, irreducibly distant, above me, a calling to which I respond, a name for my responsibility, rather than for my Being. That transcendence is engraved in the Face of the Other: for Aciman, facing Alexandria, adopting the stance of a new Passover prayer, is facing (like) a Muslim; for Lévinas, the Face of the neighbor, any neighbor, is the text of the commandment, "Thou shalt not kill," an infinite responsibility. Lévinas reads what is engraved on the Face of the Other as a "difficult freedom."[32]

*Two children dressed for bed sit on a low divan, their figures doubled* by two teddy bears strewn on the floor in front of them in the pose of displaced violence in R. B. Kitaj's first *Arabs and Jews* painting of 1985. Long in the habit of appending (sometimes affixing) commentaries to his own works, Kitaj writes: "You can choose for yourself which child is Arab and which is Jew."[33] The one looks down, chin cradled in hand, in the traditional pose of melancholy, that sense of insuperable loss, or more precisely of an endless losing that is both an acknowledgment of loss and a refusal of the consolations of finality. Eyes lowered, melancholia is to mourning as the saying to the said. And at an uneasy distance, the other looks up, looks across, finger poised at lip, uneasy, hesitating to approach, but already approaching by facing his neighbor. "Lévinas for painting. Face to Face. The Face of the Other," writes Kitaj, "Think of him as a rare Jewish angel of face-souls. Give them some visual conversation."[34]

*In a lecture series aimed at fomenting dialogue* between Israeli and American Jews, Cynthia Ozick addressed her audience at the Weizmann Institute in Israel under the heading, "Toward a New Yiddish," by which she would designate a literary language proper to Jewish writing. (But must we then call Aciman's memoir a text in the New Yiddish? Might we not equally reimagine Ozick writing, with Edmond Jabès, "Hospitality, or New Judeo-Arabic in France"?)[35] Her lecture wended its way in print from a journal of the American Jewish Congress, to a trade press publication, and on to a volume of academic essays, thus retracing the itinerary of Jewish Studies from Jewish enclave to general readership to a belated arrival in the university. On the way, Ozick shed "New Yiddish," as a figure for thinking the New as Return. But she retained the language of facing, approach, of turning *toward*. The text would eventually be titled "America: Toward Yavneh," referring to the site where, in the convulsions following the destruction of the Second Temple, textual study took up the function of (metaphorized) priestly cult. Did the ancient neighbors in Yavneh complain of secularization?

Despite the allusion to Yavneh, Ozick's predominant trope was not talmudic: "By 'centrally Jewish' I mean, for literature, whatever touches on the liturgical. Obviously this does not refer only to prayer," she writes. "In all of history the literature that has lasted for Jews has been liturgical. The secular Jew is a figment; when a Jew becomes a secular person he [*sic*] is no longer a Jew."[36] The literature that lasts for Jews, Ozick argues, is a metaphorization of liturgy.

Michael Fishbane may be understood to join the conversation, somewhere along the timeswerve. He asks, in the traditional idiom of Midrash, "To what may Scripture be likened?"[37] The process of likening is, in a different idiom, that of literary study, the process of metaphor. The rabbis do not reduce from the sacred to the secular when they interpret by likening, since this and this, this word or passage calling for exegetical comment and also this like term, this analogous passage or allegorical story that constitutes the commentary, are both the word of the tradition, and, where the teaching tradition is conceived to be unbroken, both the word of the living God.

Fishbane's question is pedagogical, not rhetorical. He teaches two answers, this and also this, which are, moreover, metaphors of one another. Like a garment, he says: "The Garments of Torah"; and also, he says, like poetry. This likening of Scripture, too, is no reduction. Rather—and this is the goal of likening—Fishbane would mark the place of Scripture, grown distant and dim for readers no longer trained (by the daily recitation of liturgy, for instance) to hear its melody, by drawing a connection to an experience that Fishbane himself imagines to be more readily available, that is the experience of the text (*textus*, the weaving, the garment) of lyric poetry. For those who continue to read "liturgical" literature, or the liturgical in literature, "ancient theophanic power of illimitable divinity may yet break through swollen words—like the raging waters of the depths that may pierce the ice-encrusted sea, as the poet Bialik imagined." Fishbane continues: "Surely we know the erupting force of new poems upon our imagination?"[38] Our reading of poems may teach us to perceive the eruptive, the uncontained and uncontainable force of the new—what literary studies call originality. How much more so, *kal ve-chomer*, or the traditional rabbinic argument a fortiori: "May we not recognize in the Bible—the foundational document of our culture—an exemplary expression of this process?"[39]

Ozick demurs. She introduces a distinction in her reply *avant la lettre* to Fishbane's metaphorization—that reply arriving along the timeswerve some two decades before his question about likening Scripture. She distinguishes, that is, between "a choral voice" and "a private voice" in lyric poetry.[40] The choral voice is more than an amplification of many private solos. Rather, the choral voice embodies the *turning toward* that Ozick refers to as "the reciprocal moral imagination."[41] If Scripture is to be likened to poetry, it is not for the eruptive force of literary originality, but rather the theophanic power is felt as a command to respond in a choral voice, to turn toward one another.

*The virtual or metaphorized dialogue* between Ozick and Fishbane is realized in a response to the literary theory of Harold Bloom, whose multi-volume project Ozick reviews some years after her visit to the Weizmann Institute, though the text of that review, "Literature as Idol," comes to share the pages of her volume *Art and Ardor* with "The New Yiddish," as though no time at all had passed between them.[42] Bloom presents originality as the prize in a contest between poets and their precursors. In one exemplification of the theory of the anxiety of influence, Bloom finds the author of the J texts of the Hebrew Scriptures to be a true original with no precursor (a poet so strong as to have eradicated any trace of prior voices);[43] which is to say that the most extreme originality can truly be likened to theophanic power.

Ozick admits Bloom's agon for writers who happen to be Jews—a self-characterization of the early Philip Roth, the strong, though slightly displaced precursor to whom Ozick had referred and with whom she wrestled in the Weizmann Institute lectures—but not for Jewish writers whose texts are centrally liturgical. She claims that Bloom's "notion of 'undoing the precursor's strength' has no validity in normative Judaism. Jewish liturgy, for instance, posits just the opposite; it posits *recapturing without revision* the precursor's stance and strength when it iterates 'our God, and God of our fathers, God of Abraham, Isaac, and Jacob.'"[44] At the primal scene of Jewish instruction, one is commanded to remember, as Yerushalmi teaches, not to revise. And taking up passages that are also keys for Yerushalmi and for Rosenzweig, she adds: "Transmittal signifies the carrying-over of the original strength, the primal monotheistic insight, the force of which drowns out competing power systems. That is what is meant by the recital in the Passover Haggadah, 'We ourselves went out from Egypt, and not only our ancestors,' and that is what is meant by the *midrash* that declares, 'All generations stood together at Sinai,' including present and future generations. In Jewish thought there *are* no latecomers."[45]

The Jewish *writer* must seek originality, but the *Jewish* writer must not. For Ozick, "if there can be such a chimera as a 'Jewish writer,' it must be the kind of sphinx or gryphon (part one thing, part another)." And referring to the midrashic account of young Abram breaking the idols of his father Terach, she adds, "Bloom himself is, sometimes purifying like

Abraham, more often conjuring like Terach, and always knowing that the two are icily, elegiacally, at war."[46]

But who slays and mourns whom? Does the Jewish *writer*, wedded to the project of originality, write an elegy for the traditionalist, left behind by modernity? Does the *Jewish* writer bury the misplaced ambitions of originality that cut off writing from its true power? And is there a harmonizing verse?

*"Two [persons appearing before a court] hold a garment.* One of them says: 'I found it,' and the other says: 'I found it'; one of them says: 'it is all mine,' and the other says: 'it is all mine,'" begins the opening mishnah of a talmudic tractate (Bava Metziah 2a). "To what may this be likened? To an encounter between the two brothers, Abraham and Tuviah Tal: 'Out of the blue you burst in,' said Tuviah," as Abraham entered the office of the family gem business. The dead father comments at the upper right margin: "It was just like Bava Metziah—just a simple tale of two people clutching at one tallis. Here, two figures are clutching one crystal."[47] The two brothers icily, elegiacally at war.

*Now definitively an exile, never to return* to the city of his birth, Benjamin writes from Paris to his dear friend Gershom Scholem in Jerusalem to request help in establishing contacts that might augment the scarce publishing opportunities for a German-speaking Jewish literary critic in Europe. In a letter of April 8, 1934, Benjamin asked Scholem to intervene with a certain Erich Reiss. Benjamin had learned in his correspondence with Theodor Adorno, already a refugee in America, that Reiss was interested in Benjamin's autobiographical text with which Scholem was familiar. Reiss was professing a Zionist line, which led Adorno to warn that there might be "certain difficulties" in securing publication, since Benjamin was no Zionist. Thus, Benjamin wrote to Scholem whose Zionist credentials were impeccable, "There might be some hope of overcoming [those difficulties] if you could point out certain *Jewish aspects* of my book, in a kind of expert's report."[48]

Scholem was more than reluctant, first, because of his strong personal distaste for Reiss, including his suspicion of Reiss's commitment to Zionism. His reply of April 19, 1934, however, focuses on the language of Benjamin's letter: "It is utterly unclear to me how you imagine I—acting as the 'expert'—could possibly discover *Zionist* elements in your book, and you will have to lend me a real hand with a list of hints."[49] Scholem's reads not—or, as Bloom would have it, misreads—"Jewish aspects," but rather "Zionist elements." It is a tendentious substitution along the bias of Scholem's own Zionist position—as though "Zionist" were coextensive with "Jewish." Scholem continues, "I don't know how you imagine what the procedure will be if you are unable to add sections that are directly relevant in *content*, not just inspired by some metaphysical *posture* . . ." (Scholem's emphases).[50] Where Benjamin is conjuring, Scholem would purify, smashing the idols of a mere posture. Having introduced "content" into the debate as an antithetical term, Scholem takes up Benjamin's key word: "You unfortunately also considerably overestimate my wisdom when you assume I could make your book's 'Jewish aspect,' which is very obscure to me, clear to a publisher."[51] It is equally tendentious to have misread Benjamin's plural "Jewish aspects," reducing them to the singular, as though only one aspect were Jewish, as though Benjamin were elevating his particular experiences as a Jew to the status of a new canon.

Writing as the posthumous editor of their joint correspondence, Scholem retroactively elucidates his objection to Benjamin's autobiographical text in a note to an earlier letter, dated January 15, 1933. Benjamin had written, "What—despite such grave faults—graced your letter in my eyes are the truly edifying and apposite sentences you write on my [unpublished 'Berlin Chronicle']"—Scholem's letter is not preserved. Benjamin continues: "'Apposite,' of course, is not meant to refer to the praise you award it, but rather to the place you reserve for this series within my work, and also to the very special thoughts you devote to the piece on 'Sexual Awakening.'"[52] Scholem appends his extensive editorial postscript at that point: "I urgently advised him to delete this section because it was the only one in the whole book in which *Jewish matters* were explicitly mentioned, thus creating the worst possible associations. There would have been no point in leaving out this section if his *Jewish experiences* had been voiced in other sections as well, but it would have been wrong to have kept it in this isolated position."[53]

But the issue of "Jewish matters" had been the very crux of the debate of content vs. aspects back when Benjamin sought Scholem's support in publishing the work. Jewish aspects of Jewish experiences, Benjamin argued, might be something other than explicit mention of "Jewish content." The Jewish matters in "Sexual Awakening," for instance, might also be read as a Jewish signature or signpost directing the reader to conjure Jewish aspects, and Jewish aspects may be precisely a non-contents, what is uncontained by the existing boundaries of any historical juncture: the new. In all its modernities, such Jewish aspects are a departure from recognizable Jewish contents, but also, on the timeswerve, an asymptotic approach ("it grew later and later without my drawing nearer the goal") toward a Jewish contents yet to come, a Saying that has not yet been Said, a difficult freedom.

---

*"Here it will not be a question of referring to Judaism,* whether traditional or modern," writes Gillian Rose in an essay celebrating the centennial of Benjamin's birth; "on the contrary, I shall propose a way of understanding the complexity of Benjamin's work which will itself yield the difficulty of his relation to Judaism."[54]

"Here"—in a new key—"it will not be"—only—"a question of referring to Judaism"—to that which is already *said* to be Judaism, to be Jewish, not only to a retrievable Jewish contents—"whether traditional or modern," Gillian Rose teaches; "on the contrary, I shall propose a way of understanding the complexity of Benjamin's work which will itself yield the *difficulty* of his relation to Judaism."

Jewish Studies as studying Jews in the difficulty of their relation, at any and perhaps every point in time, to the Tables of Jewish contents.

---

*The long deferred* face-à-face *between mother and son* in Joseph Green's Yiddish film *A Letter to Mother* produces no recognition until it is supplemented by a song.[55] The son performs an arrangement of a *niggun*—a liturgical melody, in Ozick's sense, a melody that both is and is not a prayer—that his father had invented. The father's voice, audible in the son's, is the point of continuity that turns the mother toward the son, as she rises from the audience to approach the stage.

It is *The Jazz Singer* in a new key.[56] Al Jolson's famous character Jakie is elegiacally at war with himself, jazz and kol nidre vying for his soul and, irreconcilably, for the same timeslot in his performance schedule. Jakie can do no better than alternate until the cantor-father is dead, whereupon he dons his displaced mourning as blackface, while his mother recognizes her son on the Broadway stage and applauds. In contrast, Duvid, the father and would-be cantor in *A Letter to Mother*, merges musical traditions, rather than finding himself obliged to choose between them. He overhears a non-Jewish campfire melody briefly performed on screen, intercut with a meeting on the streets of Luboml between Duvid and his young son, the latter leading a goat, a single goat. Duvid exhorts his friends and his son to stop and listen to the melody, which he immediately transposes into his *niggun*, giving the non-Jewish musical contents a Jewish aspect. Duvid's melody does not shatter the traditional Passover song of *chad gadyoh*, alluded to visually in the opening street scene, and performed at a subsequent seder scene. It widens the tent pegs. Both songs, the new and the old, have a place at the table.

———

*In a new key, one might not need to ask, which child* is Abram, which father Terach? Might one not account for their facing—now as agon, now as intimacy—as an amalgamated model of the difficulties of the field? Both-Abram-and-Terach.

To what may such a model be likened? To an ellipse. A circle has a single center; an ellipse describes a smooth orbit around two foci. The ellipse is the geometric figure of the both-and: both content and aspect, for instance. One of the foci may be invisible and yet remain a virtual center, as Severo Sarduy explicates in his phenomenology of the Baroque and Jacques Derrida in his reading of Jabès.[57] But even where the "Jewish content" is invisible to so perspicacious and well informed a scholar as Scholem, the ellipse does not necessarily collapse into a circle around the single center of assimilation to the non-Jewish world for all that, any more than the earth plunges into the sun because no visible star counterbalances its orbit.

Jewish Studies in a new key might be elliptical.

———

*"[T]he rare constellation of events* that puts a typewriter at my disposal," Benjamin reports from Paris, allows him to attempt a hasty response to Scholem on April 28, 1934. He relates that he is "preoccupied" by Scholem's most recent letter, "Intensely and sorrowfully," adding a by no means rhetorical question: "Is our understanding really threatened?"[58] The evident focus of the preoccupation, the sorrow and the threat to understanding is Scholem's disparagement of Benjamin's Marxism, but Scholem's dismissal of the theory of Jewish aspects may be read as a second, virtual focus, invisible up to the point where the draft of Benjamin's letter breaks off, except in the affect of heightened concern:

> A correspondence such as we maintain is, as you know, something very precious, but also something calling for circumspection. This circumspection by no means precludes touching on difficult questions. But these can only be treated as very private ones. To the extent that this has happened, the letters in question have definitely been filed—you can be sure of that—in my 'inner registry.' On the other hand, I sometimes get the impression that you don't raise those questions as very private ones, which they are and remain, but more as the stages of a controversy.[59]

Even the correspondence between the closest of friends requires circumspection, or, shifting geometrical and rhetorical figures, must be elliptical. The call for ellipse and ellipsis, moreover, is staged as an alternative to controversy, disputation, the violence of philosophy.

When Benjamin takes up anew his attempt to respond to Scholem across the breach in their understanding, at the jagged line of the typewritten fragment, his opening words address both the visible focus and the second, virtual center of the dispute: "This, my dear Gerhard, does not represent the first attempt to reply to your letter. But if the repeated endeavors point to a difficulty, *that difficulty does not lie in the content* of information you request, but in the form of your request. You dress it up as a—perhaps rhetorical—question: 'Is it intended to be a Communist credo?'"[60] The first half of the letter elucidates Benjamin's rejection of the political innuendo, but he finds a way beyond polemic by turning to the metaphorized prophetic eschatology that both friends recognize in Kafka, a post-prophetic counter-eschatological prophet of no-ending, of infinite approach.

Scholem has proposed a more feasible publication project on Kafka, and with Kafka in view, Benjamin abruptly changes topic and tone: "So much for your question. And this is the right point for a transition to the ideas *contained* in your letter, for which I thank you very much."[61] Benjamin welcomes the opportunity, yet still diffident with respect to *contents* he reframes the project: "but if I had to treat explicitly [Kafka's] position within Judaism, I could not do so without pointers from other parties."[62] So, it seems, polemic is not quite over, the brothers as yet at war, if less icily. To write about Kafka in a Jewish context cannot mean, for Benjamin, a facile identification of Jewish contents. In that regard he would find himself in just the same position as Scholem had claimed with respect to "the Jewish aspect" (in the singular) of Benjamin's autobiographical writing. That is, as regards Kafka, Benjamin would write instead about *the difficulty of his relation to Judaism.*

---

*Studying Jews—Bathsheba, for instance—elliptically,* Hélène Cixous's first step is to turn toward two faces in a still moment: not Bathsheba alone, but Bathsheba and her ancient maidservant in Rembrandt's painting. They are the twin centers of an orbit—youth and age, youth into age, too soon and too late, and back again. They turn away, each into her own interior, yet they also share an interior space, the intimacy of an interior: "The interior land: 'the landscape of the interior Bible.' I say the Bible, that is to say, the land of the most ancient passions, it is a land without landscape, without monuments. But not without form and without inhabitants," writes Cixous.[63] The reading of an interior Bible is an interior midrash.

Bathsheba and her maidservant do not face one another, cannot face each other. They do not speak. "They withdraw, they take their leave slowly," Cixous observes, "a thought carries them toward the unknown, far away. We hear—barely—the call from afar—" and she breaks off. We hear, but barely, we overhear a call that is not a call to us in the stillness of their faces, turned away from one another and from us. "And we, looking at them," Cixous resumes, "we see thought taking its leave." But whither the leave-taking in an interior of unbroken intimacy? "It passes," thought, that is, passes "inside, distracted, traveling, it is the foreigner, the stranger"—and another pause.[64] It is a thought that is not a retreat or retraction, but a distraction, a thinking otherwise than concentration, otherwise than circling around a single center. Thinking is the offering of hospitality to a passing thought. A thought enters our minds.

Jonathan Boyarin speaks of "Thinking in Jewish," where "Jewish" is "a partial translation, a failed translation."[65] Translating otherwise, "Thinking in Jewish" may be a thinking that passes—passes over, passes through, crosses into the land of an interior Bible—and hence might as well be "thinking in Hebrew," overhearing a partial or failed translation of *ivrit* (Hebrew), from the verb meaning to pass over from the other side.

Cixous continues, reading Rembrandt, studying Bathsheba, making her midrash, thinking in Jewish, in new Yiddish, in new Hebrew, in new Judeo-French passed over from the other side, from Algeria: "He paints the foreigner, the stranger in me, in you." A pause. "The times when under the letter's sway—." The letter sways into the picture, but Cixous remains, wills herself to be, distracted, breaks off again—then takes up that fragmenting as internal division: "We suddenly become the stranger, the foreigner in ourselves. We separate ourselves from ourselves."[66] This thinking in Jewish is not a thought of a mind-body dualism, but rather an approach to a "Thoughtful body," in particular to "A nude woman thinking," as a relation between a home and a stranger who dwells therein.[67] Thinking, in Jewish, as a thought that takes its leave, becomes a stranger, and returns to its dwelling place as a guest. Thinking of, thinking through hospitality. Jewish Studies in a new key as hospitality.

But just as Cixous takes the next step, passes over the meridian of her approach to Bathsheba, the letter returns, overcomes distraction, holds sway. "Something unreadable catches my eyes. Maybe this, I tell myself, after a long time: it is something that glides from head to toe. A motionless movement, a transformation. Now I see it, it is time, and even: it is time's writing, it is age."[68] She describes the trajectory along Bathsheba's body from "childlike" breasts to "her pelvis, her thighs, her legs," which are "in the hands of age" in more than one sense.[69] But this "ordinary metamorphosis" is still distraction.[70] And it is time for concentration, time as concentration; it is time that Cixous see the single center that would ruin her elliptical figure. "What? I mustn't say this?" she asks herself, as a strange idea passes over her into her. "But this is nonetheless what Rembrandt paints: the passion (the suffering) of Bathsheba, starts here, in the body, between the knees"—a comma, a line break—"where floats"—three dots, an ellipsis—"the letter."[71]

Later, in the twenty-fourth and final step, Cixous will say, "This is not the crucifixion."[72] Read not Christ's passion. This passion of the interior Bible—passion, patience, passivity—is also a partial or failed translation, in Jewish, a post-rabbinic midrash, of election. A metaphorization of the chosen, as the tale in the Book of Samuel—"the turning point of the whole David story," according to Robert Alter[73]—may already have been just such a metaphorization. Bathsheba has been chosen. The letter tells her so, back in step four:

The Violence of the Letter.
At first I didn't see it. The letter.
Little by little the letter captures the gazes.
At first I looked at the body.
This body that lets itself fall into itself.
That weighs. Weighing. For? Against?[74]

King David's letter, the figure of the Said, gives free rein to his passion, the violence of his passion.

Violence, the abuse of hospitality, cuts off a certain thinking—thinking as facing, thinking as Saying—and leaves, in its wake, mourning, and mourning, says Gillian Rose, becomes the law.[75]

*Two spinsters in Jerusalem, native German speakers, survivors, perhaps*, suffer the transgression of obscene phone calls. The police investigate, offer surveillance, tap the phone, but the calls continue and the spinsters feel vulnerable and sullied, especially Monika, for, as Shulamith Hareven narrates, "Monika is cleanliness itself. . . . Hence her fragrant baths three times a day."[76]

The phone rings once more during one of those baths. Eva, the second spinster, reconstructs the scene: "'She was frightened because she was naked. The phone ringing when she was naked, that's what did it."[77] Monika stood up, slipped, fell to the floor, striking her head, and died. We see the bath too soon and too late. We see that this, too, is the lasciviousness, the imperiousness of David; this, too, the story of Bathsheba and her maidservant.

Derrida, approaching Lévinas, declares: "Absolute hospitality requires that I open up my home and that I give not only to the foreigner . . . but to the absolute, unknown, anonymous other, and that I give place to them, that I let them come, that I let them arrive, and take place in the place I offer them, without asking of them either reciprocity (entering into a pact) or even their names."[78] And then turning away from Lévinas and the ethical to the "juridical-political," Derrida cautions about a "destructuration-restructuration" of the "frontier" between public space and the "at-home," which is the space of hospitality. "Now if my 'home,' in principle inviolable," he writes, "is also constituted, and in a more and more essential, interior way, by my phone line, but also by my e-mail, but also by my fax, but also by my access to the Internet, then the intervention of the State becomes a violation of the inviolable, in the place where inviolable immunity remains the condition of hospitality."[79] Under such conditions, the thinking of hospitality suffers internal division and doubling: the obscene caller and the police that tap the phone to try to catch him are the two faces of the Violence of the phone call.

*"So there is a letter," writes Cixous:*

> There is always a letter.
> The letter, what violence! How it seeks us out, how it aims at us!
> Us.
> Especially women.[80]

How it reduces the facing of two to the gaze of one.

As a last defense against the letter, violence, concentration, Cixous turns Bathsheba around, as Jonathan Boyarin says one might turn around Benjamin's angel of history by thinking in Jewish.[81] She would pass over to the other side that belongs to the night and see the unilluminated half of Bathsheba's demi-star. She follows the "two gazes," those of Bathsheba and her maidservant, as they "descend slowly, toward the bottom," beneath the floor,[82] as though the interior that they inhabit were but one focal point whose occulted twin lies in a cellar depicted in another canvas, Rembrandt's *The Slaughtered Ox*. Cixous builds a two-story house out of these canvases, likening *Bathsheba* and *The Slaughtered Ox*, as though they were text and translation, meeting at a jagged edge. Which the original, which the translation?

It is a method, a new key, this juxtaposing of canvases, of texts, where neither the apparent content, nor the historical context, underwrites the facing of texts, of canvases toward one another. In Cixous's approach, the two canvases are two stars, twin foci, or each rather "a half, a demi-star.

The other side belongs to the night"; she adds, "I will never know then but half of Bathsheba, the illuminated part."[83] Not so long as I concentrate. But if my eye wanders, if I take a sidelong glance at another demi-star, another canvas, though each is but a fragment, taken together, translations of one another, they may yet suggest the outlines of a constellation, illuminated and unilluminated, white fire on black fire.

Cixous looks aside from Bathsheba to the slaughtered ox and she sees that the one receives the metaphorized violence of the letter in her hand, and the other the unmetaphorized violence upon its butchered body. The ox opens the unilluminated interior of Bathsheba. Bathsheba faces, that is, gives a face to the ox. Is this the face on which to read Thou shalt not kill? "Bathsheba or the slaughtered ox," writes Cixous.[84] Read not "or," but rather "and also." Bathsheba and also the slaughtered ox. They cleave together and are one flesh: an ordinary translation.

*"We do not need obscure fragments* of Heraclitus to prove that being reveals itself as war to philosophical thought," Lévinas remarks, "that war does not only affect it as the most patent fact, but as the very patency, or the truth, of the real."[85] All metaphysics, all ontology, is a philosophy of war. Can Jewish Studies open its house to thinking otherwise, to thinking in peace? Can there be a practice of Jewish Studies that is not a reading and a writing of the violence of the letter? Are we under that tree yet?

Lévinas continues: "However, the extraordinary phenomenon of prophetic eschatology certainly does not intend to win its civic rights within the domain of thought by being assimilated to a philosophical evidence."[86] Like the metaphorizations of liturgy and Talmud and Midrash, there may be a prophetic eschatology in a new key whose image, too, may be shaped, may already have begun to take shape in the novelist's crucible, the painter's studio. We may already hold a key. Will we recognize a doorway to peace if we come upon it?

*Bringing together the fragments* of their interpretations of Kafka, Alter guards the peace between Scholem and Benjamin: the one taking up the role of giving pointers about Jewish contents, the other writing elliptically. Alter's explicit approach is to study their correspondence, which is to say their facing one another. Correspondence does not reduce to conflict nor to unanimity; rather it is a form of textual proximity, of intimacy, regardless of the distances that letters may traverse.

But there is another, implicit model, a Jewish aspect: Alter arranges the correspondence so that it may be likened to Talmud, as though the facing commentaries of Benjamin and Scholem were a *gemara* to Kafka as *mishnah*, that is, as the later weave of rabbinic discussion that comments upon the talmudic core. Alter's *Necessary Angels* is metaphorized Talmud, post-talmudic Talmud.

The model may be extended, the orbit enlarged. In an essay fashioned as a published correspondence, updated to the email, Jonathan Boyarin, still thinking about thinking in Jewish, sets Benjamin in the place of Kafka, and his own electronic correspondence with Martin Land as the gemara.[87] But what may be extended forward may also be extended back along the timeswerve. Benjamin's "Sexual Awakening" may enter into conversation with Bruno Schulz's "Cinnamon Shops," a fictional account of a boy sent home from the theater to fetch his father's wallet and return before the curtain might rise. The mundane errand becomes a "luminous journey" when the familiar geography of his hometown expands into "a common confusion," riddled by the temptations of art and a sexuality made more apparent in the subsequent narrative, "The Street of Crocodiles," where the contents of the cinnamon shops are revealed in the backrooms of pornography.[88]

Unknown to one another, never literally in correspondence, Benjamin and Schulz may nevertheless be overheard, in a new key, as post-rabbinic rabbis, discussing the laws of Kafka's infinite approach, of a proximity that remains a distance, of a distance that remains a form of intimacy, commentaries on Kafka's commentary: "Moses fails to enter Canaan not because his life is too short, but because it is a human life."[89] Cixous, too, joins the conversation when she writes of her emigration from her native Algeria, which, nevertheless, does not put an end to what she calls "my algeriance" as an infinite approximation: "I went toward France, without having had the idea of arriving there. Once in France I was not there. I saw that I would never arrive in France."[90] And Cixous writes back and forth along the timeswerve, rediscovers this Jewish aspect as an explicit Jewish content: "France was never the Promised Land. The sentence 'next year in Jerusalem' makes me flee."[91] Perhaps she should have vowed to face Algiers.

*"K, in Kafka's* Castle, *is my favorite Jew. Kafka is my best Jewish artist.* K never gains entry to the Castle in Kafka's book, which always lies by my bedside. There are a thousand Commentaries about this deeply Jewish book—I'd read only a few before I painted a Midrash of my own," writes Kitaj in his metaphorical midrash to his painting *K Enters the Castle at Last.*[92] He goes on to explicate the iconography of the painting in the manner of the Warburg school, which he lists, along with T. S. Eliot's notes to

his own poem, *The Waste Land*, and certain Surrealist painters, as the inspirations for his initial practice of putting "commentaries right on the pictures themselves, in writing."[93] He learns to abandon Eliot: "PAINT THE OPPOSITE OF ANTI-SEMITISM: 'The rats are underneath the piles, the jew is underneath the lot.'—T. S. Eliot / Hi, Tom. Fuck you in my art each day."[94] And following his engagement with the work of Benjamin, he finds a newness to the same, not-so-old practice: "My Commentaries—In the seventies, as my Jewish obsession began to unfold, the vast literature of Jewish commentary, exegesis and Midrash encouraged me to write about some of my pictures in a new spirit. I would put these short Jewish Commentaries next to some, not all, [of] my pictures. Make Comments New (as Jewish pomes)."[95] By this account, Kitaj's eclectic and untutored Jewish Studies was more than a transfer of a label of Jewishness to a previous practice conceived in other terms (his emphasis on the Jewishness of Warburg and Benjamin was largely the result of the later unfolding of his "Jewish obsession"). The search for a Jewish past is a means of turning toward a Jewish future.

Making commentaries and paintings both new and Jewish, Kitaj would go beyond Kafka and his commentators: "I'd like to know if any other painter or writer got K into the Castle these last 80 years. If so, please write to me," says Kitaj.[96] Show your face. Let us enter into correspondence.

Beyond the non-arrival of Cixous: beyond Benjamin's melancholia or what Rose calls *"aberrated* mourning":[97] Kitaj thinks in Jewish by painting in mystical ecstasy. Above all, he paints his deceased wife, Sandra, in present and future, no less than past, erotic embrace. That facing is depicted in *Los Angeles No. 26 (Nose Kiss)*, for instance: "This painting was inspired by an etching by the Judeophile Rembrandt, blessed be he, of two old Jews shmoozing in their Synagogue, a print of which Freud had in his consulting room," upon which he practices his ordinary metamorphosis. "The two Jews are now Sandra and me bewinged, Los Angeles," Kitaj declares, adding, with his customary insouciance, "He/I looks by chance like a cross between myself and the Lubavitcher Messiah Schneerson," and also with the seriousness of the student, "I'm still trying to solve the color in this painting, reading the section on visualization of colors in Moshe Idel's *Kabbalah*."[98]

Kitaj's messianic future is built upon a mythical past, which he paints as *Los Angeles No. 24 (Nose to Nose)*, in which his white-bearded self-portrait makes him a stand-in for Adam Kadmon, and the dark-haired Sandra is his primordial Eve. "This painting was inspired by Emmanuel Lévinas," he writes, citing Lévinas's exegesis of the ambiguity of Hebrew *tzalah* (rib, side) as the basis of his midrash to the painting. "If one sees that,"

Kitaj recites from Lévinas, "one sees that there is no longer a relation of part to whole, but a bifurcation, a division into two. One immediately sees new perspectives appear, of equality, of a same origin. I am not at all saying that the tradition of masculine domination does not exist, but that it is not the only one." Lévinas concludes, "Philosophically, the subject is not only a unity. Human subjectivity is dual. One can also wonder whether they were joined nose to nose"—which is just how Kitaj paints them.[99]

Kitaj adds a commentary on the commentary: first, some elucidation of the iconography, then these words: "Lévinas is the great philosopher of the human face. Lévinas says that God comes to him when he encounters the face of the other, even though he says that he cannot prove God's existence."[100] Proving God's existence is not the philosophical project of Lévinas, nor the painterly project of Kitaj, nor the scholarly project of Jewish Studies—but facing the Other may well be.

---

*The dual unity, face-to-face, nose-to-nose* is for Kitaj the mystical union that he learns from Scholem to call *Devekut*, cleaving, a key word for Kabbalah, and perhaps for a Jewish Studies to come.[101] "DEVEKUT!" Kitaj writes, or shouts, or blows the shofar. "This highest ideal of the mystical life, this Communion with God, seems within my reach—the reach of Jewish art no less! It goes something like this: I have come to believe fitfully"—to believe in fits and starts, discontinuously; to believe as in a fit, a paroxysm, near to madness; to believe fitfully, from an etymological root meaning "strife," to believe, therefore, strivingly, the wrestler with God—"in my Sandra as Shekhina—the female aspect of God according to Kabbalah (via Scholem)."[102] Sandra as Shekhina? Kitaj has not said, to what may she be likened? His cleaving may appear as a metaphor to the non-believer, but he may just mean it, quite literally, as mystical ecstasy. How will we know which of the words that we hear as metaphorizations today we will overhear as prayer tomorrow?

Kitaj continues his explication: "Devekut, essentially a private, ascetic communion in denial of the values of this world (I'm about to leave), is a value of contemplative, not active, social life, says Scholem. I have been slowly withdrawing from the social world for many years anyway."[103] (Kitaj seems to be unaware of Idel's breaking of Scholem's idols.)[104] A leave-taking, a withdrawal into contemplation, into thinking in Jewish, painting in Jewish: the passion of Sandra goes beyond the evisceration of the slaughtered ox, beyond the violence of any letter. Sandra Fisher or the *sheyne punim*. Kitaj faces her, both intransitively and transitively, that is both turning toward her, even in death, and giving her a face, making her face, hidden by death, visible anew, manifesting her face, the other star,

the virtual twin center, otherwise occluded, of an ellipse. "Find in painting," Kitaj exhorts and adjures, "SANDRA LOVE UNION as a Jewish
Mysticism. I mean, seek union with her in pictures. I can report some success, believe it or not."[105] Not the sacrilege of King David and the violence
of his letter—"Put Uriah in the face of the fiercest battling" (2 Sam. 11:15,
Alter's translation)—writing, in effect, thou shalt kill this man upon the
face of the husband of Bathsheba. Instead, a post-kabbalistic, but, for
Kitaj, a more than metaphorical cleaving stronger than death: he, her
dwelling place; she, his dybbuk (from the same Hebrew root, *d-v-k*, as
*devekut*), so that they become one flesh (Gen. 2:24).

Studying Jews not in the breach, but in the difficult ambiguities of
cleaving; not in the philosophical and historical evidence of unending war,
but in the conjoining of the fragments of a history of love: believe it or not.

---

*Another locksmith, another key:* Leo Gursky loves Alma and fathers her son,
but that was in the Old Country, the very old country, before, though just
before Auschwitz. And he loses his love and his son to emigration, and his
story of that love, the draft of a novel, lost, too, to the separations and
displacements, the translations and traumas of the Shoah. Until. Until
Gursky himself immigrates to America and gives up writing and takes up
the locksmith's trade. "Story of my life," says Gursky in Nicole Krauss's
*The History of Love.* "I was a locksmith. I could unlock every door in the
city. And yet I couldn't unlock anything I wanted to unlock."[106] He can
unlock his son's door, for instance, after his son's death. He can slip into
his son's brown tweed coat, hanging on the door, and into his running
sneakers. But he cannot find his own manuscript there, nor any other sign
that his son had searched for him, unlocked the secret of Gursky's fatherhood, discovered the history of love that was his history.

And yet. Until. Unless. Gursky's refrains. Unless, along the timeswerve,
the father's search for the son is the son's search for the father. Unless the
past is searching for the present, cleaving to the present, no less than the
present seeks out and cleaves to the past. Unless the history of love of
star-crossed lovers is also the eschatological prophecy of the love of father
and son, mother and daughter. Unless two roads do not diverge, and an
aged locksmith without a key and a boy without a lock, on different
quests in different books, face one another and the words of their stories
give way to the silence of their meeting.

---

*The key to rabbinic reading and to reading the rabbis, teaches Leslie Brisman, is*
*Eilu v'eilu* (Eruvin 13b): these and these, *both* the position of the house of

Hillel *and* the opposing statement of the house of Shammai, are the words of the living God.

*Eilu*, says Jonathan Safran Foer: "'If you want to come in,' he wrote"—he, the grandfather, who performs his vow of silence and communicates by writing out notes in his day book—"'we could wait for [your grandmother] together.' I asked him if he was a stranger." The question may mean, are you my thought, returning to dwell as a stranger within me? And then, as the unwitting grandson's questions continue, the undisclosed grandfather turns to a literal shorthand: "He showed me his left hand, which had YES tattooed on it. . . . He showed me his right hand, which had NO."[107]

*V'eilu*, says Nicole Krauss: when Leo Gursky finally meets his Alma, who is not the lost love of his youth, but her namesake, her revenant, ghost writer of his ghost story: "And yet. I couldn't speak. . . . She said, *The son you think didn't know—*I tapped twice."[108] The tapping is a rhythm, almost a melody, a code long since worked out with a friend and neighbor, in the Old Country and the New, a friend named Bruno, who may also be a revenant of Bruno Schulz, a code that Gursky does not disclose, does not need to disclose, to Alma, who, nevertheless, seems to "dream it to [her]self."[109] Tap three times on the pipes to ask, Are you alive? twice to answer yes, and once for no.

> She put her head on my shoulder. I tapped twice. She put her arm around me. I tapped twice. She put both arms around me and hugged me. I stopped tapping.
>
> *Alma*, I said.
> She said, *Yes*.
> *Alma*, I said again.
> She said, *Yes*.
> *Alma*, I said.
> She tapped twice.[110]

*Eilu v'eilu. This and this*, this way and also this [other] way, are the words of the living God.

"For My Grandparents," writes Krauss, in the dedication of her novel, *"who taught me the opposite of disappearing,"* the opposite of diverging, the opposite of opposing, *"and* For Jonathan, *my life,"* my cleaving unto life.

---

*An establishing shot follows two women into a Black church*, enters with them, and soon focuses on the pulpit, where Ruben, a Jewish labor organizer come from the north, in director Martin Ritt's film *Norma Rae*, addresses an integrated audience in the post- but only barely post–Jim Crow South.

"When my grandfather Abraham Isaac Warshavsky died at the age of 82, my parents attended, his brothers from Brooklyn attended, and my Aunt Minnie came up from Florida," recounts Ruben. "Also present at the funeral were 850 brothers and sisters of the United Garment Workers of America, also members of his family. They stood by him in death as in life. They earned bread together and broke bread together . . . and they were black and they were white, and they were Irish and they were Italian and they were Jews."[111] Thou shalt die, Ruben preaches, but not alone. Thou shalt be buried away, but thy face shall remain before those who live on. "But not unless you make it happen," he says, to conclude his impassioned speech, urging his audience to come and sign a union card.

Where Lévinas concentrates attention on the face of the Other, Ritt offers the counter-shot: a series of close-ups of the congregation, and they are black and they are white, and they are men and they are women. All are turned toward Ruben, attentively, keen in their listening, but the camera pauses longest on Norma Rae, who looks, but does not see, or perhaps sees, but more precisely sees through, reading his interior Bible. She had been studying Ruben for some time, but now, hearing his words, she is transfixed and transfigured. She is drawn in. It is written on her face.

Norma Rae's father will presently be murdered on screen, when, feeling the incipient signs of heart attack, he asks permission to go on an unscheduled break, and is told by the factory foreman, looking closely into his face, to go back to work. In the subsequent shot of the casket descending into the grave, Norma Rae attends, those family members previously introduced on screen attend, and some few others, but not 850 members of the non-union mill where she works, where her mother is going deaf, and where her father has just died. The scenes, in one sense, are out of order. The commentary, that is Ruben's sermon, preceded the text of her father's death. But reading otherwise, while the plot advances, the montage of scenes is a modality of the timeswerve. There is no before and after. The lesson is clear: cut to Ruben's motel room headquarters, now filled with workers, volunteering their time to help to organize the mill, and Norma Rae is ready for confrontation. And confronting management, she is ordered off the premises: an edict of expulsion.

The passion of Norma Rae: she marches into the weaving room and tries shouting her protest over the constant, deafening noise of the looms. And then she changes tactics. She contests the noise with silence. She makes a sign and stands on a table and holds it aloft for all to see. (She herself is the sign raised aloft, but " . . . no, I will not speak of this"; "this is not the crucifixion," as Cixous has said.) This is a student of Jewish Studies, who may have appeared distracted, but was taking mental notes in Ruben's class, learning to think in Jewish—even learning to speak in Jewish, to say *mensch*, to say *mitzvah*, to say *"kuv-vetch, kuv-vetch, kuv-vetch!"* enunciating two syllables a piece in a southern drawl, the new, New Yiddish. But linguistic local color is not the lesson. And Ruben himself was already speaking in translation. His word, her sign read UNION.

And looking up in a series of shot-countershot frames, one at a time, the mill workers shut down their machines. And the noise slowly diminishes and the film swerves back over movie history, returning from the talkies, first staged at the racial divide of the color line, to the silents with their title cards. And their labor ceases and there is silence, but for the hissing of the steam overhead.

*"A genuine emptiness, a pure silence are not feasible*—either conceptually or in fact," Susan Sontag argues. "If only because the artwork exists in a world furnished with many other things, the artist who creates silence or emptiness must produce something dialectical: a full void, an enriching emptiness, a resonating or eloquent silence."[112] Or, translating again with Kadya Molodowsky: "Without words, bring forth my saying."

Sontag concludes, "Silence remains, inescapably, a form of speech (in many instances, of complaint or indictment) and an element in a dialogue."[113] Inescapably. No leave-taking is complete, no complete withdrawal possible, even in the inmost interior. The practices of silence make audible a still, small voice. Traditionally, Sontag recalls, these are practices articulated in "religious vocabulary" associated with "the radical wing of the mystical tradition," whose terms she translates into the idiom of philosophy, or rather a post-philosophical thought: "As time, or history, is the medium of definite, determinate thought, the silence of eternity prepares for a thought beyond thought, which must appear from the perspective of traditional thinking and the familiar uses of the mind as no thought at all—though it may rather be the emblem of new, 'difficult' thinking"[114]—a thinking that is difficult and a thinking of the difficult, or, to configure an ahistorical constellation: read not "new, 'difficult' thinking," but, with Rosenzweig, a difficult "new thinking" that he called not an aesthetics of silence, but a "speech-thinking."[115]

Against the hissing of the steam and the ticking of the factory punch clock measuring out "homogenous, empty time,"[116] Norma Rae takes a stand upon a table. Against the violence done to laborers, she incites a work stoppage. Unless. Unless we do not know what work is.[117] Unless to stop work and to stop working is already the work to be done, the cessation of labor the work of piety. Unless the speech of silence is the broadcasting of her passion. And her passion is UNION.

Read not "union," however, but DEVEKUT.

---

Norma Rae is promptly hauled off to jail. Ruben brings her home, where her husband is anxiously waiting, and she has no more to say, at first, than that she is going to take a bath. Ritt allows her to withdraw into the interior, away from the violence of any Davidic gaze. But her husband, Sonny, wants to know why, if she had only one phone call to make, why did she call Ruben? "She knew I could make bail," he says, but Sonny is in the mood for prophecy, not jokes. What will happen? How will we go on, how will we continue to cleave to one another? How will we know what work is, which work is, for us? How will we know what we will have already begun saying before it is said? Which word will be the key? "Your wife stood on a table," Ruben tells Sonny. "She's a free woman. Either you can live with that or you can't." Live with it or not, believe it or not, face it or not.

Will Jewish Studies be a field for facing a difficult freedom? Will it be a hospitable place to take a stand for union, for the work that binds teachers and students? And can such infinite responsibility be learned, and can it be taught? And if not now, when?

---

*Will such a class, such teaching and such learning, still be Jewish Studies?*
Rosenzweig writes to Buber:

Moses' bold words, spoken to the generation who had not experienced the event of Mount Sinai (Deuteronomy 5:3), 'The Lord made not this covenant with our fathers, but with us, even us, who are all of us here alive this day,'—those words (the paradox of which was keenly felt by ancient commentators) had fallen into oblivion. It is upon us to accept the challenge of this boldness. The inner line of demarcation has become blurred, and there must be an outer one, for not every deed which fails to find its place in the law known to us broadens it boundaries, as not every piece of our knowledge becomes a part of the *teaching*. But we cannot know whether it will not happen after all. We do not know the boundary, and we do not know how far the pegs of the tent of the Torah may be extended, nor which one of our deeds is destined to accomplish such widening. We may be sure that they are being extended through us; for could anything be allowed to remain outside permanently?[118]

# Notes

INTRODUCTION

1. Franz Rosenzweig, "Upon Opening the *Jüdisches Lehrhaus*: Draft of an Address," in *On Jewish Learning*, ed. N. N. Glatzer (Madison: University of Wisconsin Press, 2002), 95.

2. Ibid.

3. Jacob Neusner, *Jerusalem and Athens: The Congruity of Talmudic and Classical Philosophy* (Leiden: Brill, 1997), x.

4. Talal Asad, *Formations of the Secular: Christianity, Islam, Modernity* (Stanford, Calif.: Stanford University Press, 2003), 47.

5. Danièle Hervieu-Léger, *Religion as a Chain of Memory*, trans. Simon Lee (New Brunswick, N.J.: Rutgers University Press, 2000), 67.

6. Mordecai M. Kaplan, *Judaism as a Civilization: Toward a Reconstruction of American-Jewish Life* (1934; reprint, New York: Schocken Books, 1967), 431.

7. Dan Miron, *The Image of the Shtetl and Other Studies of Modern Jewish Literary Imagination* (Syracuse: Syracuse University Press, 2000), 21.

8. Ibid., 33.

9. Paul Ricoeur, *The Rule of Metaphor* (Toronto: University of Toronto Press, 1975), see esp. 7.

10. David G. Roskies, "S. Ansky and the Paradigm of Return," in *The Uses of Tradition: Jewish Continuity in the Modern Era*, ed. Jack Wertheimer (New York: Jewish Theological Seminary, 1992), 258.

11. Eugene M. Avrutin and Harriet Murav, "Introduction: Photographing the Jewish Nation," in *Photographing the Jewish Nation: Pictures from S. An-sky's Ethnographic Expeditions*, ed. Eugene M. Avrutin, Valerii Dymshits, Alexander Ivanov, Alexander Lvov, Harriet Murav and Alla Sokolova (Waltham, Mass.: Brandeis University Press; Hanover, N.H.: University Press of New England, 2009), 10.

12. Peter Burke, *The French Historical Revolution: The Annales School, 1929–1989* (Stanford, Calif.: Stanford University Press, 1990), 67.

13. The selections are also guided by practical considerations: in almost all cases, citations refer to works in English, for accessibility (translations duly noted, otherwise my own) and limited to book publications. Also, the notes are all but exclusively limited to providing bibliographical information on works cited, rather

than, for instance, surveying the list of further studies germane to the points under discussion.

14. Jorge Luis Borges, "The Garden of Forking Paths," trans. Donald A. Yates, in *Labyrinths: Selected Stories and Other Writings*, ed. Yates and James E. Irby (New York: New Directions, 1964), 28.

15. See, for instance, Enrique Dussel, *Ethics and the Theology of Liberation*, trans. Bernard F. McWilliams (Maryknoll, N.Y.: Orbis, 1978), 28–29.

16. See Paul Gilroy, *The Black Atlantic: Modernity and Double Consciousness* (London: Verso, 1993); Sander L. Gilman, *Multiculturalism and the Jews* (New York: Routledge, 2006).

17. Charles Bernstein, "Time Out of Motion: Looking Ahead to See Backward," in *A Poetics* (Cambridge, Mass.: Harvard University Press, 1992), 120n22.

18. Andrew Bush, "Teaching Continually: Beginning with Lévinas," in *Europe and Its Boundaries: Words and Worlds, Within and Beyond*, ed. Andrew Davison and Himadeep Muppidi (Lanham, Md.: Lexington Books, Rowman and Littlefield, 2009), 5–23.

19. Walter Benjamin, "Thought-Figures," trans. Rodney Livingston, in *Selected Writings*, gen. ed. Michael W. Jennings, vol. 2, *1927–1934*, ed. Michael W. Jennings, Howard Eiland, and Gary Smith (Cambridge, Mass.: Belknap Press, Harvard University Press, 1999), 726.

20. Walter Benjamin, "Goethe's Elective Affinities," trans. Stanley Corngold, in *Selected Writings*, gen. ed. Michael W. Jennings, vol. 1, *1913–1926*, ed. Marcus Bullock and Michael W. Jennings (Cambridge, Mass.: Belknap Press, Harvard University Press, 1996), 298.

CHAPTER 1 — TERMS OF DEBATE

1. Hannah Arendt, *Rahel Varnhagen: The Life of a Jewess*, ed. Liliane Weissberg, trans. Richard and Clara Winston (Baltimore: Johns Hopkins University Press, 1997).

2. Ibid., 85.

3. Emily D. Bilski and Emily Braun, eds., *Jewish Women and Their Salons: The Power of Conversation* (New York: The Jewish Museum; New Haven, Conn.: Yale University Press, 2005).

4. Barbara Hahn, *The Jewess Pallas Athena: This Too a Theory of Modernity*, trans. James McFarland (Princeton, N.J.: Princeton University Press, 2005), 48.

5. Ibid.

6. Derek Penslar, *Shylock's Children: Economics and Jewish Identity in Modern Europe* (Berkeley: University of California Press, 2001); and Yuri Slezkine, *The Jewish Century* (Princeton, N.J.: Princeton University Press, 2004), 9.

7. Glückel of Hameln, *The Memoirs of Glückel of Hameln*, trans. Marvin Lowenthal (New York: Schocken, 1977).

8. Marion A. Kaplan, *The Making of the Jewish Middle Class: Women, Family, and Identity in Imperial Germany* (New York: Oxford University Press, 1991).

9. George L. Mosse, "Jewish Emancipation: Between *Bildung* and Respectability," in *The Jewish Response to German Culture: From the Enlightenment to the Second World War*, ed. Jehuda Reinharz and Walter Schatzberg (Hanover, N.H.: University Press of New England, 1985), 2.

10. Arendt, *Rahel Varnhagen*, 29.

11. Hahn, *The Jewess Pallas Athena*, 76.

12. Gayatri Spivak, "Can the Subaltern Speak?," in *Marxism and the Interpretation of Culture*, ed. Cary Nelson and Lawrence Grossberg (Urbana: University of Illinois Press, 1988).

13. Sander L. Gilman, *Multiculturalism and the Jews* (New York: Routledge, 2006), 27.

14. Karl Jaspers, quoted in Heidi Thomann Tewarson, *Rahel Levin Varnhagen: The Life and Work of a German Jewish Intellectual* (Lincoln: University of Nebraska Press, 1998), 4.

15. Ibid.

16. Arendt, *Rahel Varnhagen*, 187.

17. Ibid., 85.

18. Hannah Arendt, "The Jew as Pariah: A Hidden Tradition," in *The Jew as Pariah: Jewish Identity and Politics in the Modern Age*, ed. Ron H. Feldman (New York: Grove, 1978), 67–90.

19. Arendt, *Rahel Varnhagen*, 85.

20. Ruth Wisse, *The Shlemiel as Modern Jewish Hero* (Chicago: University of Chicago Press, 1971), 4.

21. Arendt, "The Jew as Pariah," 68.

22. Hannah Arendt, *Eichmann in Jerusalem: A Report on the Banality of Evil* (New York: Penguin, 1977); Berel Lang, *Heidegger's Silence* (Ithaca, N.Y.: Cornell University Press, 1996).

23. Steven E. Aschheim, ed., *Hannah Arendt in Jerusalem* (Berkeley: University of California Press, 2001); also Aschheim, *Scholem, Arendt, Klemperer: Intimate Chronicles in Turbulent Times* (Bloomington: Indiana University Press; Cincinnati: Hebrew Union College—Jewish Institute of Religion, 2001), and Aschheim, *Beyond the Border: The German-Jewish Legacy Abroad* (Princeton, N.J.: Princeton University Press, 2007).

24. Charles Taylor, *Sources of the Self: The Making of the Modern Identity* (Cambridge, Mass.: Harvard University Press, 1989).

25. Moses Hess, *The Revival of Israel: Rome and Jerusalem, The Last National Question*, trans. Meyer Waxman (Lincoln: University of Nebraska Press, 1995), 35.

26. Ibid., 128.

27. Ibid., 106.

28. Ibid., 92.

29. Ken Koltun-Fromm, *Moses Hess and Modern Jewish Identity* (Bloomington: Indiana University Press, 2001), 59.

30. Hess, *The Revival of Israel*, 36.

31. Ibid., 69.

32. Henrietta Herz, *Ihr Leben und ihr Zeit*, ed. Hans Landsberg (Weimar: G. Kiepenheuer, 1913), 100, emphasis added.

33. Hess, *The Revival of Israel*, 38.

34. Wilhelm von Humboldt, "The Task of the Historian," in Leopold Ranke, *The Theory and Practice of History*, ed Georg G. Iggers and Konrad von Moltke, trans. Wilma A. Iggers and Konrad von Moltke (Indianapolis: Bobbs-Merrill, 1973), 6.

35. Isaac Marcus Jost, "Rigors of Jewish Historiography," in *Ideas of Jewish History*, ed. Michael A. Meyer (New York: Behrman House, 1974), 183.

36. Immanuel Kant, "Answer to the Question: What is Enlightenment?," trans. Thomas K. Abbott, in *Basic Writings of Kant*, ed. Allen W. Wood (New York: Modern Library, 2001), 133–141.

37. Note the late effort to refute the "documentary hypothesis" on behalf of the unity of the revealed text in the work of Jewish biblical scholar Umberto Cassuto, *The Documentary Hypothesis and the Composition of the Pentateuch: Eight Lectures*, trans. Israel Abrahams (Jerusalem: Magnes Press, Hebrew University, 1961).

38. Jost, "Rigors of Jewish Historiography," 184.

39. Ibid.

40. Heinrich Graetz, *History of the Jews*, 6 vols., trans. Bella Löwy (Philadelphia: Jewish Publication Society, 1891–1898).

41. Heinrich Graetz, "The Structure of Jewish History," in Graetz, *The Structure of Jewish History*, ed. and trans. Ismar Schorsch (New York: Jewish Theological Seminary, 1975), 65–66.

42. Ibid., 69.

43. Graetz, *History of the Jews*, 1:1.

44. Chana Kronfeld, "Beyond Deleuze and Guattari: Hebrew and Yiddish Modernism in the Age of Privileged Difference," in *Jews and Other Differences: The New Jewish Cultural Studies*, ed. Jonathan Boyarin and Daniel Boyarin (Minneapolis: University of Minnesota Press, 1997), 261.

45. Hess, *The Revival of Israel*, 121.

46. Ibid., 78.

47. Ibid., 165.

48. Koltun-Fromm, *Moses Hess*, 59.

49. Samson Raphael Hirsch, *The Nineteen Letters on Judaism*, ed. Jacob Breuer, trans. Bernhard Drachman (New York: Feldheim, 1969), 25.

50. Ibid., 29.

51. Daniel Boyarin, *Unheroic Conduct: The Rise of Heterosexuality and the Invention of the Jewish Man* (Berkeley: University of California Press, 1997).

52. Hirsch, *The Nineteen Letters*, 113.

53. Ibid., 99.

54. Ibid.

55. Hess, *The Revival of Israel*, 43.

56. Ibid., 44.

57. Ibid., 45.

58. Ibid., 46.

59. Ibid., 44.

60. Ibid., 47.

61. Ibid., 65.

62. Arendt, "'Eichmann in Jerusalem': Exchange of Letters Between Gersholm Scholem and Hannah Arendt," in *The Jew as Pariah*, 240–251.

63. Gershom Scholem, "Reflections on Modern Jewish Studies," in *On the Possibility of Jewish Mysticism in Our Time and other Essays*, ed. Avraham Shapira, trans. Jonathan Chipman (Philadelphia: Jewish Publication Society, 1997), 51n.

64. Ibid., 54–55.

65. Ibid., 58.

66. Leopold Zunz, "On Rabbinic Literature," in *The Jew in the Modern World: A Documentary History*, ed. Paul R. Mendes-Flohr and Jehuda Reinharz (New York: Oxford University Press, 1980), 222.

67. Ibid.

68. C. H. Kraeling, "The Synagogue," in *The Excavations at Dura-Europas Conducted by Yale University and the French Academy of Inscriptions and Letters: Preliminary Report of Sixth Season of Work, October 1932–March 1933*, ed. M. I. Rostovtzeff, A. R. Bellinger, C. Hopkins, and C. B. Welles (New Haven, Conn.: Yale University Press, 1936), 382.

69. Lawrence Schiffman, *Reclaiming the Dead Sea Scrolls* (Philadelphia: Jewish Publication Society, 1994), 3–58.

70. Hayim Nahman Bialik and Yehoshua Hana Ravnitsky, eds., *The Book of Legends/ Sefer Ha-Aggadah: Legends from the Talmud and Midrash*, trans. William G. Braude (New York: Schocken, 1992).

71. David Stern, "Introduction," in Bialik and Ravnitsky, *The Book of Legends*, xvii–xviii.

72. Bialik and Ravnitsky, *The Book of Legends*, 406.

73. Louis Ginzburg, *The Legends of the Jews*, trans. Henrietta Szold (Philadelphia: Jewish Publication Society, 1909–1938).

74. Zunz, "On Rabbinic Literature," 222.

75. Ibid., emphasis added.

76. Scholem, "Reflections," 59.

77. Michael Waszynski, dir., *Der Dibuk/The Dybbuk* (Waltham, Mass.: National Center for Jewish Film, 1991); and S. Ansky, *The Dybbuk and Other Writings*, ed. David G. Roskies, trans. Golda Werman. (New Haven, Conn.: Yale University Press, 2002).

78. Scholem, "Reflections," 59.

79. Harold Bloom, *The Anxiety of Influence: A Theory of Poetry* (Oxford: Oxford University Press, 1973), 139–155; and Bloom, *Kabbalah and Criticism* (New York: Seabury, 1975).

80. David G. Roskies, *The Jewish Search for a Usable Past* (Bloomington: Indiana University Press, 1999), 1–16.

81. David Biale, *Gershom Scholem: Kabbalah and Counter-History* (Cambridge, Mass.: Harvard University Press, 1979), 102.

82. Ibid.

83. Susannah Heschel, *Abraham Geiger and the Jewish Jesus* (Chicago: University of Chicago Press, 1998), 14.

84. Ibid., 10.

85. Abraham Geiger, "The Developing Idea," in Meyer, *Ideas of Jewish History*, 164.

86. Ibid.

87. Heschel, *Abraham Geiger*, 14.

88. Ibid., 15.

89. See David N. Myers, *Resisting History: Historicism and Its Discontents in German-Jewish Thought* (Berkeley: University of California Press, 2003).

90. Scholem, "Reflections," 69.

91. Salo Wittmayer Baron, *A Social and Religious History of the Jews*, 6 vols. (New York: Columbia University Press, 1952–1993).

92. Michael A. Meyer, *Jewish Identity in the Modern World* (Seattle: University of Washington Press, 1990), 5.

93. Ibid., 39.

94. Salo Wittmayer Baron, *The Jewish Community: Its History and Structure to the American Revolution* (Philadelphia: Jewish Publication Society, 1942), 1:12.

95. Ibid., 1:29.

96. Ibid., 1:3.

97. Todd M. Endelman, *The Jews of Georgian England, 1714–1830: Tradition and Change in a Liberal Society* (Philadelphia: Jewish Publication Society, 1979).

98. Endelman's subtitle openly alludes to Jacob Katz, *Tradition and Crisis: Jewish Society at the End of the Middle Ages*, trans. Bernard Dov Cooperman (Syracuse, N.Y.: Syracuse University Press, 2000).

99. Endelman, *The Jews of Georgian England*, 6.

100. Yosef Kaplan, *An Alternative Path to Modernity: The Sephardic Diaspora in Western Europe* (Leiden: Brill, 2000), esp. 26–28.

101. Dipesh Chakrabarty, *Provincializing Europe: Postcolonial Thought and Historical Difference* (Princeton, N.J.: Princeton University Press, 2000), 6.

102. Ammiel Alcalay, "Exploding Identities: Notes on Ethnicity and Literary History," in *Jews and Other Differences*, 330–344.

103. Ibid., 332–333.

104. Robert Alter, quoted in ibid., 338.

105. Alcalay, "Exploding Identities," 338–339.

106. Ismar Schorsch, *From Text to Context: The Turn to History in Modern Judaism* (Waltham, Mass.: Brandeis University Press; Hanover, N.H.: University Press of New England, 1994), 71–92.

107. Ivan Davidson Kalmar and Derek J. Penslar, eds., *Orientalism and the Jews* (Waltham, Mass.: Brandeis University Press, 2005).

108. Steven E. Aschheim, *Brothers and Strangers: The East European Jew in German and German Jewish Consciousness, 1800–1923* (Madison: University of Wisconsin Press, 1982); Elizabeth Friedman, *Colonialism and After: An Algerian Jewish Community* (South Hadley, Mass.: Bergin and Garvey, 1988).

109. Friedman, *Colonialism and After*, 8.

110. Olga Bush, "The Architecture of Jewish Identity: The Neo-Islamic Central Synagogue of New York," *Journal of the Society of Architectural Historians*, 61:2 (2004): 180–201.

111. Ivo Andric, quoted in Alcalay, "Exploding Identities," 342.

112. Alcalay, "Exploding Identities," 343.

113. Rabbi David d'Beth Hillel, *Unknown Jews in Unknown Lands: The Travels of Rabbi David d'Beth Hillel (1824–1832)*, ed. Walter J. Fischel (New York: Ktav, 1973).

114. Paolo Bernardini and Norman Fiering, eds., *The Jews and the Expansion of Europe to the West, 1450–1800* (New York: Berghahn Books, 2001).

115. José Amador de los Ríos, *Estudios históricos, políticos y literarios sobre los judíos de España* (Madrid: M. Díaz, 1848), xx.

116. José Amador de los Ríos, *Historia social, política y religiosa de los judíos de España y Portugal* (Madrid: T. Fortanet, 1875–1876), 17.

117. Ibid., 22.

118. Amador de los Ríos, *Estudios*, 650–651.

119. Immanuel Wolf, "On the Concept of the Science of Judaism," in Mendes-Flohr and Reinharz, *The Jew in the Modern World*, 194.

120. Américo Castro, *The Structure of Spanish History*, trans. Edmund L. King (Princeton, N.J.: Princeton University Press, 1954).

121. Ibid., 528.

122. Ibid., 46.

123. For a recent example, see Jerrilynn D. Dodds, Maria Rosa Menocal, and Abigail Krasner Balbale, *The Arts of Intimacy: Christians, Jews, and Muslims in the Making of Castilian Culture* (New Haven, Conn.: Yale University Press, 2008).

124. Castro, *The Structure of Spanish History*, 191.

125. Benzion Netanyahu, "The Racial Attack on the Conversos," in *Toward the Inquisition: Essays on Jewish and Converso History in Late Medieval Spain* (Ithaca, N.Y.: Cornell University Press, 1997), 1–42.

126. Yitzhak Baer, *A History of the Jews in Christian Spain*, 2 vols., trans. Louis Schoffman (Philadelphia: Jewish Publication Society, 1961).

127. A counter-paradigm is now gaining prominence in Ashkenazi studies, as discussed in and exemplified by Benjamin Nathans, *Beyond the Pale: The Jewish Encounter with Late Imperial Russia* (Berkeley: University of California Press, 2002).

128. Mark R. Cohen, *Under Crescent and Cross: The Jews in the Middle Ages* (Princeton, N.J.: Princeton University Press, 1994).

129. For an overview, see Norman A. Stillman, "The Judeo-Arabic Heritage," in *Sephardic and Mizrahi Jewry: From the Golden Age of Spain to Modern Times*, ed. Zion Zohar (New York: New York University Press, 2005), 40–54.

130. For instance, David M. Gitlitz, *Secrecy and Deceit: The Religion of the Crypto-Jews* (Philadelphia: Jewish Publication Society, 1996); and, more recently, Yirmiyahu Yovel, *The Other Within: The Marranos: Split Identity and Emerging Modernity* (Princeton, N.J.: Princeton University Press, 2009).

131. Frédéric Brenner, *Les derniers marranes / The Last Marranos* (Waltham, Mass.: National Center for Jewish Films, 1990).

132. Henry Kamen, *The Spanish Inquisition: A Historical Revision* (London: Weidenfeld and Nicolson, 1997), 37; and Baer, *A History*, 2:424.

CHAPTER 2 — STATE OF THE QUESTION

1. Lucy S. Dawidowicz, *The War Against the Jews: 1933–1945* (New York: Holt, Rinehart and Winston, 1975).

2. Elie Wiesel, *Night*, trans. Stella Rodway, in *Night/Dawn/Day* (Northvale, N.J.: Jason Aronson, 1985), 72.

3. Walter Benjamin, "On the Concept of History," trans. Harry Zohn, in Benjamin, *Selected Writings, 1938–1940*, ed. Howard Eiland and Michael W. Jennings (Cambridge, Mass.: Belknap Press, Harvard University Press, 2003), 391.

4. Ibid., 390.

5. Yehuda Bauer, *Rethinking the Holocaust* (New Haven, Conn.: Yale University Press, 2001).

6. Deborah E. Lipstadt, *Denying the Holocaust: The Growing Assault on Truth and Memory* (New York: Free Press, 1993), 220.

7. Raul Hilberg, *The Destruction of the European Jews*, rev. ed., 3 vols. (New York: Holmes and Meier, 1985).

8. Bauer, *Rethinking the Holocaust*, 119–166.

9. Steven Spielberg, dir., *Schindler's List* (Universal City, Calif.: Universal, 1993).

10. Primo Levi, "Shame," in *The Drowned and the Saved*, trans. Raymond Rosenthal (New York: Summit, 1988), 70–87; and Giorgio Agamben, *Remnants of Auschwitz: The Witness and the Archive*, trans. Daniel Heller-Roazen (New York: Zone Books, 1999).

11. Emil L. Fackenheim, *The Jewish Return into History: Reflections in the Age of Auschwitz and a New Jerusalem* (New York: Schocken, 1978), 22. Emphasis in the original.

12. Claude Lanzmann, dir., *Shoah* (New York: New Yorker Video, 1999).

13. Eric R. Wolf, *Europe and the People without History* (Berkeley: University of California Press, 1982).

14. Adam Czerniakow, *The Warsaw Diary of Adam Czerniakow: Prelude to Doom*, ed. Raul Hilberg and Stan and Josef Kermisz, trans. Staron and Yad Vashem (New York: Stein and Day, 1978).

15. The Shoah Visual History Foundation (1994), now USC Shoah Foundation Institute for Visual History and Education.

16. Raul Hilberg, ed., *Documents of Destruction: Germany and Jewry, 1933–1945* (Chicago: Quadrangle, 1971).

17. Lucy S. Dawidowicz, ed., *A Holocaust Reader* (New York: Behrman House, 1976), x.

18. Theodor W. Adorno, *Prisms*, trans. Samuel and Shierry Weber (Cambridge, Mass.: MIT Press, 1981), 34.

19. Theodor W. Adorno, *Negative Dialectics*, trans. E. B. Ashton (New York: Seabury, 1973), 361–362.

20. Theodor W. Adorno, "Education After Auschwitz," trans. Rodney Livingston, in *Can One Live After Auschwitz?: A Philosophical Reader*, ed. Rolf Tiedemann (Stanford, Calif.: Stanford University Press, 2003), 19–35.

21. Paul Ritterband and Henry S. Wechsler, *Jewish Learning in American Universities: The First Century* (Bloomington: Indiana University Press, 1994), 216.

22. Ibid.

23. E.g., Simon M. Dubnow, *History of the Jews in Russia and Poland, from the Earliest Times until the Present Day*, trans. I. Friedlaender, 3 vols. (Philadelphia: Jewish Publication Society, 1916–1920); and Emmanuel Ringelblum, *Notes from the Warsaw Ghetto: The Journal of Emmanuel Ringelblum*, ed. and trans. Jacob Sloan (New York: McGraw-Hill, 1958).

24. Franz Rosenzweig, "The Builders: Concerning the Law," in *On Jewish Learning*, ed. N. N. Glatzer (Madison: University of Wisconsin Press, 2002), 82.

25. Ibid., emphasis added.

26. Erik H. Erikson, *Identity: Youth and Crisis* (New York: W. W. Norton, 1994), 17.

27. Caroline Walker Bynum, *Metamorphosis and Identity* (New York: Zone, 2001), 163.

28. Ibid.

29. Fredrik Barth, ed., *Ethnic Groups and Boundaries: The Social Organization of Culture Difference* (Bergen-Oslo: Universitets Forlaget, 1969).

30. S. Ilan Troen, "The Construction of a Secular Jewish Identity: European and American Influences in Israeli Education," in *Divergent Jewish Cultures: Israel and America*, ed. Deborah Dash Moore and S. Ilan Troen (New Haven, Conn.: Yale University Press, 2001), 28.

31. Zalman Aranne, quoted in Troen, "The Construction of a Secular Jewish Identity," 28, emphasis added.

32. Troen, "The Construction of a Secular Jewish Identity," 45.

33. Ibid., 46.

34. George Devereux, "Ethnic Identity: Its Logical Foundations and Its Dysfunctions," in *Ethnic Identity: Cultural Continuities and Change*, ed. George De Vos and Lola Romanucci-Ross (Palo Alto, Calif.: Mayfield Publishing, 1975), 53.

35. Shaye J. D. Cohen, *The Beginnings of Jewishness: Boundaries, Varieties, Uncertainties* (Berkeley: University of California Press, 1999).

36. Ibid., 3.

37. Amos Funkenstein, *Perceptions of Jewish History* (Berkeley: University of California Press, 1993), 14.

38. Tamar Garb, "Modernity, Identity, Textuality," in *The Jew in the Text*, ed. Linda Nochlin and Tamar Garb (London: Thames and Hudson, 1995), 29.

39. Linda Nochlin, "Starting with the Self: Jewish Identity and Its Representations," in *The Jew in the Text*, ed. Nochlin and Garb, 14.

40. Cohen, *The Beginnings of Jewishness*, 6.

41. Ibid., 59.

42. Eric M. Meyers, "Aspects of Everyday Life in Roman Palestine with Special Reference to Private Domiciles and Ritual Baths," in *Jews in the Hellenistic and Roman Cities*, ed. John R. Bartlett (London: Routledge, 2002), 197.

43. Doron Mendels, *Identity, Religion and Historiography: Studies in Hellenistic History* (Sheffield, Eng.: Sheffield Academic Press, 1998), 20.

44. Cohen, *The Beginnings of Jewishness*, 346.

45. David G. Roskies, "The Jewish Search for a Usable Past," in *The Jewish Search for a Usable Past* (Bloomington: Indiana University Press, 1999), 1 and 10.

46. Ibid., 10.

47. Maurice Samuel, *The World of Sholom Aleichem* (New York: Knopf, 1943).

48. Renée Levine Melammed, *A Question of Identity: Iberian Conversos in Historical Perspective* (Oxford: Oxford University Press, 2004), viii.

49. Ibid.

50. Penslar, *Shylock's Children*, 60–61.

51. Ibid., 61.

52. Ibid., 61–62, emphasis added.

53. Martin Jay, *The Dialectical Imagination: A History of the Frankfurt School and the Institute for Social Research, 1923–1950* (Boston: Little, Brown, 1973), 34.

54. Marla Brettschneider, "To Race, to Class, to Queer: Jewish Contributions to Feminist Theory," in *Jewish Locations: Traversing Racialized Landscapes*, ed. Lisa Tessman and Bat-Ami Bar-On (Lanham, Md.: Rowman and Littlefield, 2001), 213–238.

55. Barbara A. Holdrege, "Beyond Hegemony: Hinduisms, Judaisms, and the Politics of Comparison," in *Indo-Judaic Studies in the Twenty-first Century: A View from the Margin*, ed. Nathan Katz, Ranabir Chakravarti, Braj M. Sinha, and Shalva Weil (New York: Palgrave Macmillan, 2007), 77–78.

56. Marla Brettschneider, "Theorizing Identities as Mutually Constitutive: A Critical Reading of Spelman, Aristotle and Jewish Law," in *Feminist Politics: Identity, Difference, and Agency*, ed. Deborah Orr, Dianna Taylor, Eileen Kahl, Kathleen Earle, Christa Rainwater, and Linda López McAlister (Lanham, Md.: Rowman and Littlefield, 2007), 185–211.

57. Sara Horowitz, "Jewish Studies as Oppositional? or Gettin' Mighty Lonely Out Here," in *Styles of Cultural Activism: From Theory and Pedagogy to Women, Indians, and Communism*, ed. Philip Goldstein (Newark: University of Delaware Press; London: Associated University Presses, 1994), 152–164.

58. See the more recent book by Melanie Kaye/Kantrowitz, *The Color of Jews: Racial and Radical Diasporism* (Bloomington: Indiana University Press, 2007).

59. Sandi Simcha Dubowski, dir., *Trembling Before G-d* (New York: New Yorker Video, 2003).

60. Rabbi Rachel Adler, *Engendering Judaism: An Inclusive Theology and Ethics* (Philadelphia: Jewish Publication Society, 1998), 50.

61. Brettschneider, "To Race, to Class, to Queer," 214–215.

62. Ibid., 215.

63. Ibid., 216.

64. Daniel Boyarin, *Unheroic Conduct: The Rise of Heterosexuality and the Invention of the Jewish Man* (Berkeley: University of California Press, 1997), 116.

65. Marvin Fox, *Interpreting Maimonides: Studies in Methodology, Metaphysics, and Moral Philosophy* (Chicago: University of Chicago Press, 1990), 22.

66. Ibid., 72–73.

67. Maimonides, quoted in Fox, *Interpreting Maimonides*, 76.

68. Brettschneider, "To Race, to Class, to Queer," 225.

69. Ibid., 218.

70. Pierre Bourdieu, *Outline of a Theory of Practice*, trans. Richard Nice (New York: Cambridge University Press, 1977).

71. Moshe Idel, *Kabbalah: New Perspectives* (New Haven, Conn.: Yale University Press, 1988), 27.

72. Steven J. Zipperstein, *Imagining Russian Jewry: Memory, History, Identity* (Seattle: University of Washington Press, 1999), 57.

73. Ibid., 48.

74. See Maurice Halbwachs, *On Collective Memory*, ed. and trans. Lewis A. Coser (Chicago: University of Chicago Press, 1992).

75. Jan Assman, *Religion and Cultural Memory*, trans. Rodney Livingstone (Stanford, Calif.: Stanford University Press, 2006), 93.

76. Yosef Hayim Yerushalmi, *Zakhor: Jewish History and Jewish Memory* (Seattle: University of Washington Press, 1996).

77. Ibid., 44.

78. David N. Myers, "Of Marranos and Memory: Yosef Hayim Yerushalmi and the Writing of Jewish History," in *Jewish History and Jewish Memory: Essays in Honor of Yosef Hayim Yerushalmi*, ed. Elisheva Carlebach, John M. Efron, and David N. Myers (Hanover, N.H.: Brandeis University Press, University Press of New England, 1998), 1–21.

79. Yosef Hayim Yerushalmi, *From Spanish Court to Italian Ghetto: Isaac Cardoso, A Study in Seventeenth-Century Marranism and Jewish Apologetics* (New York: Columbia University Press, 1971), 34.

80. Abraham Ibn Daud, *Sefer Ha-Qabbalah: The Book of Tradition*, ed. and trans. Gerson D. Cohen (Oxford: Littman Library of Jewish Civilization, 2005).

81. Gerson D. Cohen, "The Blessing of Assimilation in Jewish History," in *Understanding Jewish Theology: Classical Issues and Modern Perspectives*, ed. Jacob Neusner (New York: Ktav, Anti-Defamation League of B'nai Brith, 1973), 251–258.

82. Cohen, in Ibn Daud, *Sefer Ha-Qabbalah*, 189.

83. Ibid., 189.

84. Ibid., 180, emphasis added.

85. Ibid., 190.

86. Idel, *Kabbalah*, 14.

87. Cohen, in Ibn Daud, *Sefer Ha-Qabbalah*, 189.

88. Idel, *Kabbalah*, 6.

89. Cohen, in Ibn Daud, *Sefer Ha-Qabbalah*, 190–191.

90. Ibid., lvii.

91. Ibid.

92. S. D. Goitein, *A Mediterranean Society: The Jewish Communities of the Arab World as Portrayed in the Documents of the Cairo Geniza*, 6 vols. (Berkeley: University of California Press, 1967–1993).

93. Ibid., 5: xix.

94. Ibid., 4:84.

95. Ibid., 4:82.

96. Ibid., 5:6.

97. Ibid., 4:82.

98. See, for instance, James Clifford and George E. Marcus, eds., *Writing Culture: The Poetic and Politics of Ethnography* (Berkeley: University of California Press, 1986).

99. Marc Kaminsky, "A Table with People: Storytelling as Life Review and Cultural History," in *YIVO Annual* 21: *Going Home*, ed. Jack Kugelmass (Evanston, Ill.: Northwestern University Press; New York: YIVO Institute for Jewish Research, 1993), 87–131; Ruth Behar, "Death and Memory: From Santa María del Monte to Miami Beach," in *The Vulnerable Observer: Anthropology That Breaks Your Heart* (Boston: Beacon, 1996), 34–89; and Jonathan Boyarin, "Waiting for a Jew: Marginal Redemption at the Eighth Street Shul," in *Thinking in Jewish* (Chicago: University of Chicago Press, 1996), 8–33.

100. Pierre Nora, "Between Memory and History: *Les Lieux de Mémoire*," trans. Marc Roudebush, *Representations* 26 (1989): 7–25.

101. Irving Howe, *World of Our Fathers* (New York: Harcourt Brace Jovanovich, 1976); Anita Shapira, *Land and Power: The Zionist Resort to Force, 1881–1948* (New York: Oxford University Press, 1992); and Joëlle Bahloul, *The Architecture of Memory: A Jewish-Muslim Household in Colonial Algeria 1937–1962*, trans. Catherine du Péloux Ménagé (Cambridge: Cambridge University Press, 1996).

102. Irving Howe and Eliezer Greenberg, eds., *A Treasury of Yiddish Stories* (New York: Viking, 1954); Irving Howe and Eliezer Greenberg, eds., *A Treasury of Yiddish Poetry* (New York: Schocken, 1969).

103. Howe, *World of Our Fathers*, xix.

104. Ibid., 39.

105. Ibid., 144, emphasis added.

106. Shapira, *Land and Power*, 106.

107. Yael Zerubavel, *Recovered Roots: Collective Memory and the Making of Israeli National Tradition* (Chicago: University of Chicago Press, 1995), 147-177.

108. Aharon Sher quoted in Shapira, *Land and Power*, 99.

109. Shapira, *Land and Power*, 108-109.

110. Ibid., 109.

111. Ibid., 209 and 116.

112. Ibid., 107.

113. Ibid., vii.

114. Howe, *World of Our Fathers*, 605.

115. Ibid., 604.

116. Ibid., 604-605.

117. Ibid., emphasis added.

118. Ibid., 607.

119. Bahloul, *The Architecture of Memory*, 126.

120. Ibid., 126.

121. Elliot R. Wolfson, *Language, Eros, Being: Kabbalistic Hermeneutics and Poetic Imagination* (New York: Fordham University Press, 2005), xx.

122. Ibid., 214.

123. Bahloul, *The Architecture of Memory*, 129.

124. Ibid., 41.

125. Ibid.

126. Ibid., 42.

127. Halbwachs, *On Collective Memory*, 105-106.

128. Bahloul, *The Architecture of Memory*, 42.

129. Cynthia Baker, *Rebuilding the House of Israel: Architectures of Gender in Jewish Antiquity* (Stanford, Calif.: Stanford University Press, 2002).

130. Ibid., 126.

131. Yosef Hayim Yerushalmi, "Postscript: Reflections on Forgetting," in Yerushalmi, *Zakhor*, 113.

132. Funkenstein, *Perceptions of Jewish History*, 16.

133. Ibid., 16–17.

134. Ibid., 18.

135. Ibid., 19.

136. Ibid., 25.

137. Ibid., 11.

138. Ibid., 25.

139. Jacob Neusner, *A History of the Mishnaic Law of Purities: Kelim* (Leiden: Brill, 1974), part 1, xi.

140. Especially Jacob Neusner, *Eliezer ben Hyrcanus: The Tradition and the Man* (Leiden: Brill, 1973).

141. Neusner, *A History of the Mishnaic Law*, part 1, xi.

142. Daniel Boyarin, *Intertextuality and the Reading of Midrash* (Bloomington: Indiana University Press, 1990), 14.

143. Neusner, *A History of the Mishnaic Law*, part i, xi, emphasis added.

144. Ibid., part 1, xii.

145. Ibid., part. 1, xiv.

146. Ibid., part 1, xvii.

147. Ibid., part 3, 273.

148. Ibid., part 3, 273.

149. Ibid., part 1, xvi.

150. Ibid., part 3, 273.

151. Ibid., part 3, 274.

152. Judith Plaskow, *Standing Again at Sinai: Judaism from a Feminist Perspective* (San Francisco: Harper, 1991), 35.

153. Chava Weissler, *Voices of the Matriarchs: Listening to the Prayers of Early Modern Jewish Women* (Boston: Beacon Press, 1998), 51–65.

154. Elisheva Baumgarten, *Mothers and Children: Jewish Family Life in Medieval Europe* (Princeton, N.J.: Princeton University Press, 2004), 12.

155. David Biale, ed., *Cultures of the Jews: A New History* (New York: Schocken, 2002).

156. Lucette Valensi, "Multicultural Visions: The Cultural Tapestry of the Jews of North Africa," in Biale, *Cultures of the Jews*, 896.

157. Marc S. Bernstein, *Stories of Joseph: Narrative Migrations between Judaism and Islam* (Detroit: Wayne State University Press, 2006), 11.

158. Among the cognates, consider "boundaries," as seen in the subtitle of Shaye Cohen's *The Beginnings of Jewishness*, and "frontier," as in Jonathan Ray, *The Sephardic*

*Frontier: The* Reconquista *and the Jewish Community in Medieval Iberia* (Ithaca, N.Y.: Cornell University Press, 2006).

159. Michael Taussig, *Mimesis and Alterity: A Particular History of the Senses* (New York: Routledge, 1993).

160. Paula E. Hyman, *The Emancipation of the Jews of Alsace: Acculturation and Tradition in the Nineteenth Century* (New Haven, Conn.: Yale University Press, 1991).

161. Sarah Abrevaya Stein, *Making Jews Modern: The Yiddish and Ladino Press in the Russian and Ottoman Empires* (Bloomington: Indiana University Press, 2004), 189.

162. Ibid., 190–191.

163. Ruth Wisse, *The Modern Jewish Canon: A Journey through Language and Culture* (New York: Free Press, 2000), e.g., 6.

164. Ibid., 84.

165. Ibid.

166. Ibid., 15.

167. Benjamin Harshav, "The Modern Jewish Revolution," in *Language in Time of Revolution* (Berkeley: University of California Press, 1993), 3–77; following Itamar Even-Zohar, "Aspects of the Hebrew-Yiddish Polysystem: A Case of a Multilingual Polysystem," *Poetics Today* 11:1 (1990): 121–130.

168. Wisse, *The Modern Jewish Canon*, 18.

169. Ibid., 5.

170. Susan Gubar, *Poetry after Auschwitz: Remembering What One Never Knew* (Bloomington: Indiana University Press, 2003), xv.

CHAPTER 3 — IN A NEW KEY

1. André Aciman, *Out of Egypt: A Memoir* (New York: Riverhead, 1994), 339.

2. Franz Rosenzweig, "The Builders: Concerning the Law," in *On Jewish Learning*, ed. N. N. Glatzer (Madison: University of Wisconsin Press, 2002), 72.

3. Martin Buber, "*Herut*: On Youth and Religion," trans. Eva Jospe, in *On Judaism*, ed. Nahum N. Glatzer, trans. Eva Jospe et al. (New York: Schocken, 1967), 149, quoting Pirke Avoth 6:2.

4. Rosenzweig, "The Builders," 72.

5. Yosef Hayim Yerushalmi, "Postscript: Reflections on Forgetting," in *Zakhor: Jewish History and Jewish Memory* (Seattle: University of Washington Press, 1996), 113.

6. Edmond Jabès, *Le livre de l'hospitalité* (Paris: Gallimard, 1991), 13.

7. Benjamin Zucker, "Guide to the Reader," appearing in both *Blue: A Novel* (Woodstock, N.Y.: Overlook, 2000), vii; and *Green: A Novel* (Woodstock, N.Y.: Overlook, 2002), vii.

8. Zucker, *Green*, 85.

9. Zucker, "Guide"; see Elliot R. Wolfson, *Language, Eros, Being: Kabbalistic Hermeneutics and Poetic Imagination* (New York: Fordham University Press, 2005), xx, discussed above, chapter 2.

10. Zucker, *Green*, 85.

11. Ibid.

12. Ibid., 43.

13. Ibid.

14. Ibid.

15. S. Y. Agnon, *A Guest for the Night*, trans. Misha Louvish (New York: Schocken, 1968), 95.

16. Ibid.

17. Ibid., 98.

18. Ibid.

19. Ibid.

20. Jehuda Halevy, "Between East and West," trans. Barbara Galli (following Rosenzweig's translation) in Barbara Ellen Galli, *Franz Rosenzweig and Jehuda Halevi: Translating, Translations, and Translators* (Montreal: McGill-Queen's University Press, 1995), 146; and Rosenzweig, "Notes," in Galli, *Franz Rosenzweig and Jehuda Halevi*, 264.

21. Jonathan Safran Foer, *Everything Is Illuminated* (New York: Perennial/ HarperCollins, 2003).

22. Jonathan Safran Foer, *Extremely Loud & Incredibly Close* (Boston: Houghton Mifflin, 2005), 302, 304; the intervening page 303 is taken up by a photo of a key.

23. Robert Frost, "Two Roads Diverged," in *Collected Poems, Prose and Plays* (New York: Library, 1995), 103.

24. Benjamin, "Berlin Childhood Around 1900," trans. Howard Eiland, in *Selected Writings*, gen. ed. Michael W. Jennings, vol. 3, *1935–1938*, ed. Howard Eiland and Michael W. Jennings (Cambridge, Mass.: Belknap Press, Harvard University Press, 2002), 344.

25. Ibid.

26. Benjamin, "The Task of the Translator," trans. Harry Zohn, in *Selected Writings*, gen. ed. Michael W. Jennings, *1913–1926*, ed. Marcus Bullock and Michael W. Jennings (Cambridge, Mass.: Belknap Press, Harvard University Press, 1996), 260.

27. Benjamin, "A Berlin Chronicle," trans. Edmund Jephcott, in *Selected Writings*, *1927–1934*, ed. Michael W. Jennings, Howard Eiland, and Gary Smith (Cambridge, Mass.: Belknap Press, Harvard University Press, 1999), 629–630.

28. Aciman, "Alexandria: The Capital of Memory," in *False Papers: Essays on Exile and Memory* (New York: Farrar, Straus, Giroux, 2000), 3.

29. Emmanuel Lévinas, *Outside the Subject*, trans. Michael B. Smith (Stanford, Calif.: Stanford University Press, 1994), 51.

30. Lévinas, *Otherwise than Being; or, Beyond Essence*, trans. Alphonso Lingis (The Hague: M. Nijhoff, 1981), 5–6.

31. Kadya Molodowsky, "Without Words," in *Paper Bridges: Selected Poems of Kadya Molodowsky*, ed. and trans. Kathryn Hellerstein (Detroit: Wayne State University Press, 1999), 438–439.

32. Lévinas, "Education and Prayer," in *Difficult Freedom: Essays on Judaism*, trans. Seán Hand (Baltimore: Johns Hopkins University Press, 1990), 272.

33. Kitaj, "Second Diasporist Manifesto," in *R. B. Kitaj: How to Reach 72 in a Jewish Art, including the Second Diasporist Manifesto* (New York: Marlborough, 2005), 24.

34. Ibid., 11.

35. See Cynthia Ozick, "Envy; or Yiddish in America," in *The Pagan Rabbi and Other Stories* (New York: E. P. Dutton, 1983), 39–100; and Jabès, *Le livre de l'hospitalité*.

36. Ozick, "Toward a New Yiddish," in *Art and Ardor* (New York: Knopf, 1983), 169.

37. Michael Fishbane, "The Garments of Torah—Or, to What May Scriptures Be Compared?" in *The Garments of the Torah: Essays in Biblical Hermeneutics* (Bloomington: Indiana University Press, 1989), 33–46.

38. Ibid., 129.

39. Ibid.

40. Ozick, "Toward a New Yiddish," 169.

41. Ibid.

42. Ozick, "Literature as Idol: Harold Bloom," in *Art and Ardor*, 178–199. For the works under review, see especially Harold Bloom, *The Anxiety of Influence: A Theory of Poetry* (New York: Oxford University Press, 1973); also Bloom, *Kabbalah and Criticism* (New York: Seabury, 1975).

43. Harold Bloom and David Rosenberg, *The Book of J* (New York: Grove Weidenfeld, 1990).

44. Ozick, "Literature as Idol," 194.

45. Ibid.

46. Ibid., 198.

47. Zucker, *Blue*, 21.

48. Walter Benjamin, *The Correspondence of Walter Benjamin and Gershom Scholem, 1932–1940*, ed. Gershom Scholem, trans. Gary Smith and Andre Lefevere (New York: Schocken, 1989), 106, emphasis added.

49. Scholem, in Benjamin, *Correspondence*, 107.

50. Ibid.

51. Ibid.

52. Benjamin, *Correspondence*, 25.

53. Scholem, in Benjamin, *Correspondence*, 25n, emphases added.

54. Gillian Rose, "Walter Benjamin—Out of the Sources of Modern Judaism," in *Judaism and Modernity: Philosophical Essays* (Oxford: Blackwell, 1993), 177.

55. Joseph Green, dir., *A Letter to Mother/A Brivele der Mamen*, Green-Film, 1938 (restoration, Teaneck, N.J.: Ergo Media, 1997).

56. Alan Crosland, dir., *The Jazz Singer*, Warner Brothers/Vitaphone, 1927 (Burbank, Calif.: Warner Home Video, 2007).

57. Severo Sarduy, *Barroco: Ensayos generales sobre el barroco* (Buenos Aires: Sudamericana, 1974); Derrida "Ellipsis," in *Writing and Difference*, trans. Alan Bass (Chicago: University of Chicago Press, 1978), 295–300.

58. Benjamin, *Correspondence*, 108.

59. Ibid., 109.

60. Ibid., emphasis added.

61. Ibid., 111, emphasis added.

62. Ibid.

63. Hélène Cixous, "Bathsheba or the Interior Bible," trans. Catherine A. F. MacGillvray, in *Stigmata: Escaping Texts* (London: Routledge, 1998), 6.

64. Ibid., 9.

65. Jonathan Boyarin, "Introduction," in *Thinking in Jewish* (Chicago: University of Chicago Press, 1996), 1.

66. Cixous, "Bathsheba," 9.

67. Ibid., 10.

68. Ibid., 11–13. (In the midst of the quotation, page 12 is occupied by the reproduction of a drawing by Rembrandt that Cixous relates to his *Bathsheba*.)

69. Ibid.

70. Ibid., 17.

71. Ibid., 13.

72. Ibid., 23.

73. Robert Alter, *The David Story: A Translation and Commentary of 1 and 2 Samuel* (New York: Norton, 1999), 249n.

74. Cixous, "Bathsheba," 13.

75. Gillian Rose, *Mourning Becomes the Law: Philosophy and Representation* (Cambridge: Cambridge University Press, 1996).

76. Shulamith Hareven, *Twilight and Other Stories*, trans. Miriam Arad, Hillel Halkin, J. M. Lask, and David Weber (San Francisco: Mercury House, 1992), 63.

77. Ibid., 67.

78. Jacques Derrida, "Foreigner Question," trans. Rachel Bowlby, in Derrida and Anne Dufourmantelle, *Of Hospitality* (Stanford, Calif.: Stanford University Press, 2000), 25.

79. Ibid., 51.

80. Cixous, "Bathsheba," 14.

81. J. Boyarin, "Introduction," 6.

82. Cixous, "Bathsheba," 11.

83. Ibid., 23.

84. Ibid.

85. Emmanuel Lévinas, *Totality and Infinity; an Essay on Exteriority*, trans. Alphonso Lingis (Pittsburgh: Duquesne University Press, 1969), 5.

86. Ibid., 7.

87. See Jonathan Boyarin, "A Moment of Danger, a Taste of Death," in *Jewishness and the Human Dimension* (New York: Fordham University Press, 2008), 89–114.

88. Bruno Schulz, "Cinnamon Shops," in *The Street of Crocodiles*, trans. Celina Wieniewska (Harmondworth, Eng.: Penguin, 1977), 96; see also "The Street of Crocodiles," 99–110, and Kafka, "A Common Confusion," trans. Will and Edwin Muir in *The Complete Stories*, ed. Nahum N. Glatzer (New York: Schocken, 1971), 429–430.

89. Kafka, *Diaries, 1914–1923*, ed. by Max Brod, trans. Martin Greenberg, with the co-operation of Hannah Arendt (New York: Schocken, 1965), 196.

90. Cixous, "My Algeriance, in other words: to depart not to arrive from Algeria," trans. Eric Prenowitz, in *Stigmata*, 226.

91. Ibid., 227.

92. Kitaj, *R. B. Kitaj: How to Reach 72*, 57.

93. Kitaj, "Manifesto Continued: A Personal Theory of Jewish Art (A User's Manual)," in ibid., 13.

94. Ibid., 12.

95. Ibid., 15.

96. Ibid., 42.

97. Rose, "Walter Benjamin," 209.

98. Kitaj, *R. B. Kitaj: How to Reach 72*, 57; see Moshe Idel, *Kabbalah: New Perspectives* (New Haven, Conn.: Yale University Press, 1988).

99. Kitaj, *R. B. Kitaj: How to Reach 72*, 49.

100. Ibid.

101. Scholem, "Devekut, or Communion with God," in *The Messianic Idea in Judaism and Other Essays on Jewish Spirituality* (New York: Schocken, 1971), 203–227.

102. Kitaj, "Manifesto Continued," 10.

103. Ibid.

104. Idel, "Varieties of Devekut in Jewish Mysticism," in *Kabbalah*, 35–58.

105. Kitaj, "Manifesto Continued," 10.

106. Nicole Krauss, *The History of Love* (New York: Norton, 2005), 122.

107. Foer, *Extremely Loud*, 237–238.

108. Krauss, *History*, 252.

109. Kafka, "An Imperial Message," trans. Willa and Edwin Muir, in *Complete Stories*, 5.

110. Krauss, *History*, 252.

111. Martin Ritt, dir., *Norma Rae* (Twentieth Century–Fox, 1979; Farmington Hills, Mich.: CBS Fox Video, 1985).

112. Susan Sontag, "The Aesthetics of Silence," in *Styles of Radical Will* (New York: Delta / Dell, 1970), 11.

113. Ibid., 21.

114. Ibid., 17.

115. Franz Rosenzweig, "'The New Thinking': A Few Supplementary Remarks to *The Star* [*of Redemption*]," in *Franz Rosenzweig's 'The New Thinking*," ed. and trans. Alan Udoff and Barbara E. Galli (Syracuse, N.Y.: Syracuse University Press, 1999), 67–102.

116. Benjamin, "On the Concept of History," trans. Harry Zohn, in *Selected Writings*, gen. ed. Michael W. Jennings, *1938–1940*, ed. Howard Eiland and Michael W. Jennings (Cambridge, Mass.: Belknap Press, Harvard University Press, 2003), 396.

117. See Philip Levine, *What Work Is* (New York: Knopf, 2004), 18–19.

118. Rosenzweig, "The Builders," 87.

# Index

# About the Author

Andrew Bush received his Ph.D. in comparative literature at Yale University in 1983 and has taught ever since at Vassar College, where, for the past ten years, he has divided his teaching evenly between the Department of Hispanic Studies and the Jewish Studies Program. He is the author of many essays in those fields and of *The Routes of Modernity: Spanish American Poetry from the Early Eighteenth to the Mid-Nineteenth Century*.